GOAT

GOAT

A Story of Kashmir & Notting Hill

JUSTINE HARDY

JOHN MURRAY
Albemarle Street, London

© Justine Hardy 2000

First published in 2000
by John Murray (Publishers) Ltd,
50 Albemarle Street, London W1X 4BD

The moral right of the author has been asserted

A catalogue record for this book is available from the British Library

ISBN 0-7195-6145 0

Typeset in 11.5/14 Goudy by Servis Filmsetting Ltd, Manchester
Printed and bound in Great Britain by the University Press, Cambridge

For my mother and father with love

Contents

CHAPTER 1

Abdullah
the Storyteller

THE SMELL OF crushed green cardamom reminds me of English lawns and wood smoke with an edge of ginger, faintly erotic but remote. In a small room in a dark shop on a back street in Delhi, cinnamon and cloves were being ground up with the cardamom. Together they recalled Christmases past. But it was July, high summer in the choking downtown area of the Indian capital, every sound except the grinding of spices deadened by the torpor of midday.

'My name is Abdullah Awqaf. I am from Srinagar.'

The Kashmiri who had beckoned me from his shop next to the spice merchant looked down the swoop of his nose with eyes the colour of Nagin Lake in May.

'But now I am Abdullah of Jor Bagh market, New Delhi, and on this day you have been sent to my shop, *inshallah*, God willing.' He settled himself cross-legged in the middle of the room, drew his palms together and began his sales song.

'Are you feeling much of cold?' he asked.

'Not at this moment,' I replied. Even the backs of my hands were sweating.

'But there must be times when you are having of cold?' he pressed, swatting the heavy air.

'In the winter.'

'Ah.' He rolled the sound from his throat, the Kashmiri sales-man's call to prayer. 'Then it is time for you to have pashmina.'

This was why I had come to Jor Bagh market.

'Pash what?' Innocence was written all over my face.

'I will have to tell you a story.' Abdullah sank his hands into the folds of his *feron*, his long tunic. 'Have you been to Kashmir?'

'No,' I lied.

'It is so beautiful, incredible.' He twitched the tip of his nose. 'We have a bird in my valley. It is all the colours of the sun and the rain. The name in your language means bird of paradise. You know paradise?'

'I hope to go.'

He smiled. '*Inshallah*, we will all be visiting. Our bird of para-dise must be coming from there. It is so rare, you understand?'

'Of course.'

'My grandfather was finding a way to catch these birds. I am not lying to you. These birds were flying into his hands.'

Of course he was not lying to me.

'And the feathers, so beautiful you cannot imagine, incredible. My grandfather was weaving these feathers together, making shawls from the sun and the rain, what is it you call it? Yes, rainbow, that is it.' His hands came from the depths of his *feron* and took flight with his fancy. 'Pashmina.' His eyes were no longer focusing.

'Do you have some that I could see?' I asked.

'But of course.' And he called one of his boys down from the room above.

The tale of the birds of paradise had been set against the quiet bubbling of prayer from the top of a ladder leading to an upper room above the shop. One of the faithful appeared, wearing white *kurta pyjama* and Nike trainers. He slid down the ladder with a bundle wrapped in calico under one arm. Abdullah the storyteller rolled up his sleeves and untied the knots, his eyes half-closed in

2

reverence. Out of the bundle flew his birds – flights of turquoise, fuchsia and imperial purple. He whirled them around his head and I reached out to touch one. It blew into my face like down, its softness somewhere between childhood and rose petals. Of course it was not made from feathers. It came from a goat.

I had come to Jor Bagh market to buy pashmina because I had had an idea. At Abdullah's shop I spent two months' rent on four shawls and then I wrote to my old friend Robin in England who had been in the wool trade for forty years.

Abdullah's small shop in the market was on the corner of a street next to a spice merchant whose beard was dyed the same colour as his orange lentils. A pavement magazine-seller had his wares laid out between the two shops, his posters of smouldering Bollywood film stars on the spice merchant's side of the pavement and the magazines on Abdullah's side. On the way past I had seen a fairly new copy of *Vogue* lined up between a finger-waving politician on the front of a news magazine and a copy of *Here's Health* (special infertility supplement free). The paper-*wallah* had sold it to me at an inflated price, though he did offer to throw in *Here's Health* as well.

The *Vogue* cover girl had been a beautiful Englishwoman from Lahore, her newborn son on her hip. He was wrapped in a pashmina shawl. Not very many people knew what pashmina was then, in the days before it was so liberally draped around the shoulders of the great and the glittering in the world of high fashion. Then, pashmina had been the preserve of Indian women and a few frequent visitors to the subcontinent who had discovered the rose-petal kiss of the mountain goats. But I had had an idea. If pashmina had appeared on the cover of *Vogue*, then it wouldn't be long before the ladies-who-lunch of Notting Hill would be wanting it too, in every colour that Abdullah the storyteller had ever dreamt of. And if I were to sell them the shawls, I knew too where I'd send the profit.

Two years earlier, in 1996, I had gone to work for an Indian newspaper in Delhi. In October the following year I was sent out to the slums to interview a man. His name was Gautam Vohra and he had given up his career to set up schools in the slums. I was thorough in my research and I went with him to all of the areas where he had started schools. As I did so I watched him and wondered why a man at the height of his career as a national newspaper editor and television personality had given it all up to work for no pay among the disenfranchised and dispossessed of Delhi.

When the heat was not so destructive and autumn mellowed the sun, when the children climbed over him and his smile illuminated his whole face, the 'why' seemed irrelevant. But when, in the depths of winter, he bumped up and down the roads to the slums, past pockets of shops where the slum landlords beat money out of their tenants, past groups of children carrying sagging plastic bags full of tin cans and rags picked from the city's dumps, past layers of oppressive greyness, then it was hard to understand how he could have given up his other life.

My research trips had carried on through the winter as I gathered material for a series of articles about NGOs, non-government organizations. I made my sixth slum visit with Gautam on a day in December when the fog of pollution was so thick that we had to drive with the headlights on at two in the afternoon. The sun was just a smudge through the yellowing layers that sat over the city.

Part of the way through that visit Gautam sat in the doorway of a house, looking in on one of the adult education classes. Though it was bitterly cold, he did not try to go into the house. The class was for women and taught by women. It was for those who wanted to learn to read and write Hindi. Most of the slum dwellers come from different states, converging on Delhi in search of hope, only to be met by millions of others doing the same. They speak different languages, they follow different gods. Hindi gives them a voice in the capital, a chance to fight against poverty and exploitation.

The women were squatting among the shadows of the window-less room. I crouched among them, trying to ignore the spreading cramp in one foot that was about to topple me into a woman in a pea-green sari next to me. They were singing. The song was part of the lesson and a way of remembering the Hindi alphabet for a people more familiar with song than with the word on the page. I tried to sing as well. They winced but smiled. Some half hid their faces behind chiffon. They had pulled their sari ends over their faces when Gautam came to the door, as they always had in their villages when a man who was not from their family was near. The older women and I were bare-faced, they excused by age, I by other conventions.

Gautam stood up to move on. The women reached out to me in farewell and I reached back. Touch is their language, woman to woman.

I followed Gautam to a courtyard where, under a *keekar* tree, he talked to a boy in a rumpled uniform. The boy's blue shorts were held up by a striped and elasticated belt, its buckle a looped snake. I had had a belt like that once when I was his age. It had seemed to represent all things adult and modern. He pulled it out from his shorts and let it snap back. I used to do that too, even though it hurt. Everyone who had one of those belts used to snap them. Gautam fluffed the boy's hair as the belt thwacked against his narrow belly.

'You know that you are part of the family of DRAG now?' Gautam looked at the boy as he spoke.

DRAG stood for Development Research and Action Group, the rather dour title of Gautam's NGO. The boy looked up, his head on one side, his foot rolled in. He had not understood. Gautam had spoken in English.

'Are you talking to me?' I asked.

'I do not think our young friend has much English as yet.'

'What do you mean "a part of the family"?' I reached out my hand to the boy. He ducked away and ran out on to the road, shouting to three friends who had been studiously pushing sticks through the rusty spokes of a dead bicycle.

Gautam laughed.

'It may take some of them a little longer to get used to you.'

'I still don't see why I am a member of the family. What family?'

'You have been to all the slums now. That is more than one has to do for research. There is more to it than that. Am I right?'

So he had noticed. He put his hand into the small of my back to guide me away from a handcart. It was being pushed by a man with just a whorl of scar tissue where his left eye had once been. The one that remained was fixed on his merchandise – acid-bright plastic puppies with nodding heads and wagging tails. The manoeuvre around the man gave me a moment to respond.

'What you do here is extraordinary. I am trying to understand it.'

'One is not doing any more than one can.' He used 'one' like the Queen and my grandfather, the formality maintaining the distance between us. He added to it by taking his hand away as he side-stepped some splattered cow dung.

'You seem to care about them.' He had put his hands in his pockets.

'How could you not?'

'Millions don't.' He dug his hands deeper into his pockets.

'But there can't be very much someone like me can do. I can hardly even communicate with them. We only speak to each other in Hindi and though we are all pretty bad, I'm by far the worst.'

'You can help us to get money. We need money.'

Of course he needed money. Is there a charity or a non-government organization anywhere that does not need money? Gautam's role in his organization had been born out of a growing anger with the Indian establishment. He came from it himself but he raged at what he saw as its criminal lethargy in claiming to run the largest democracy in the world whilst depriving the majority of those people of the basic right to an education.

There was nothing that I could usefully say. I was not in a position to write a cheque. Neither did I believe that I would get much response to pleas on behalf of an Indian-based organization if I got up on a soap box in London and started to spout about the basic right of every human being to have some kind of formal education. I did not want to give my hero a cynical-sounding response so I retreated into silence. He in turn was quiet.

The fog clung. None of the children that normally make up the small groups hanging around the streets were about, just a bald dog with sores down its serrated spine picking through a pile of rubbish in search of food. There wasn't any. There is no waste in the slums.

We turned a corner to where Gautam had left his jeep. A small girl was sitting alone on the doorstep of a grey house. She was wearing a thin dress, its hem fraying around her shins, but her hair, in two neat plaits, had been tied tight with polka-dot ribbons. She was wrapped in a bright orange shawl, vivid amidst her grey concrete surroundings.

Then the idea came. If I sold shawls it would be a way of making some of the money that Gautam needed. It would be so simple. I knew I could do it. I had already made my first sale without even trying a few weeks earlier, on a brief trip to London.

It had been cold too in Notting Hill. People on the street had surprised expressions, caught out by the first frost. They scuttled along, looking up at the sky just to check that it really was as bleak as it felt. The beautiful but weary were making their way to a popular café to while away the long hours until another evening's entertainment began.

I was not looking my best. The back of my grey tracksuit resembled the sagging folds of an elephant's bottom. My gym shoes were a memento of an inter-school netball tournament *circa* 1982. The one redeeming feature of my ensemble was a pashmina shawl. It was the colour of flame-tree flowers and it had been given to me by a houseboat owner in Kashmir with whom I had stayed years before. I had become immediately attached to it without really knowing anything about pashmina.

As the Notting Hill rain started, I retreated into the folds of my shawl and took refuge in the doorway of a post office. Inside a woman in a tight white jersey was shrieking at a man behind one of the glass serving screens, telling him that he had absolutely no idea about service. He didn't seem to mind, happy, perhaps, just to admire the sharp nipples that the tight white jersey showed off so nicely. Its wearer abandoned her tirade and came towards me.

'Can you believe how rude some people are?' she said in Manhattan Islandese.

I smiled back at her.

'That shawl, I want it. Where did you get it?'

'From Kashmir.'

'Belief.' She pulled one end of the shawl towards her.

'I must have one.'

I looked at her.

'Oh, forget my manners. It's a New York thing. Let me buy it from you.'

I couldn't think of anything to say.

'Come on, how much is it? I have cash, I'll pay you right now.'

'£200.'

The shawl was four years old – £50 a year seemed reasonable.

'Great.'

She tugged more forcefully at the dangling end of the shawl. It fell free, aflame at her feet. She picked it up, twined it around her neck and grabbed my hand, pulling me down the street. We stopped in the rain outside an antique shop with a French mirror in the window, one of those ones that have reflected the image of a thousand courtesans. The American twirled in front of the glass.

Godson Digby, an early convert to my importing pashmina

'I love it, I love it.' She opened her bag. 'Now, what about a discount?'

'Please, may I have my shawl back?'

I remember holding out my hand.

'Come on,' she wheedled.

'If you would like it I have told you how much it is, otherwise please may I have it back?'

She pushed four £50 notes into my hand and walked away.

She had managed to make me feel like a drug-dealer, but it had been my first sale. I was not going to have to try very hard to sell pashmina. And by the time I had the idea of using shawls to raise money for education in the slums, *Vogue* was setting up the shoot with the baby from Lahore: the fashion world was about to discover pashmina.

As my plan evolved over the months I decided to photograph shawls on some of the children whom I had met on my visits with Gautam. The slums as a backdrop would be too raw, too unpalatable for the *Vogue*-buying tastes of the West. The children were beautiful, uncomplicated models who would look straight into the camera. Surely it would not be offensive if I used some of the children to model the shawls, in a setting that would give people images of India, without smacking them in the face with battered reality.

On a July afternoon in 1998 I took four boys, a girl and the four shawls that I had recently bought from Abdullah to the gardens where the Sayyid and Lodi rulers are buried under curvaceous domes in elegant Delhi.

I had met the children in one of the slums. I had gone there without Gautam because I was not sure he would understand my motive. I had to pay the taxi-driver three times the usual waiting charge to get him to stay while I went to try and find children.

Whenever I had been out in the slums before there seemed to be children everywhere. Now the pitted alleys were empty. The sun was still trying to fight its way through the smog. I could only see dogs without flesh or fur hunched beside a *nala*, an open sewer, where filth was fermenting. I did not want to walk too far. Every alley seemed the same.

Then the sun broke through the haze and children appeared. Five came towards me from beside a boarded and padlocked shop advertising cures for 'haemorrhoids and all matters pustular', four brothers and their little sister.

'Would you like to spend an afternoon in Lodi Gardens?' If I had asked five children the same question in any area of London I would have been arrested.

The four boys kicked stones in the dust. The little girl asked me why.

'I have some beautiful shawls that I would like to photograph and I think you would make them look . . .'

What would they make them look like? Slum children draped in expensive shawls amidst the Bollywood curves of fifteenth- and sixteenth-century Mogul tombs? That wasn't what I wanted. I wanted to try and catch their sense of fun, their ability to laugh and play for hours with things that they had made themselves out of the rubbish they found in the streets, cars made of old wire, spinning tops that had once been *ghee* tins. I hoped they would be able to play with the shawls.

'I think you would make them look alive.'

They stopped kicking stones and looked at me. The middle-sized boy stepped towards me.

'You want pictures of beggars. We are not beggars. Our father is working in a factory. He is making plastic bags.' He looked straight at me as he spoke.

I looked away.

'I know you are not beggars. I don't want to photograph beggars. I would like to take pictures of you in the shawls for fun.'

'Why?' asked the tallest boy.

'Because . . . I have a taxi waiting. We will go to the gardens in a taxi and I will bring you back in a taxi . . . '

'Okay, we are coming,' the little girl interrupted before I had finished.

The promise of a taxi ride had sealed it.

The four boys spread themselves across the back seat and the little girl sat on my lap in the front. She fiddled with the things I was wearing, particularly an old rose quartz rosary that I wore around my wrist.

'What is this?' she asked, as we bounced along the road away from the slums.

'I use it to meditate.' And I mumbled the first line of one of the meditations that I had been taught by a man with a large stomach and a serene smile.

She threw her little head back and laughed. Then she passed the information on to her brothers in the back seat. They sat in silence as we drove towards imperial Delhi, Lutyens to the left in the sweep and roll of government buildings, India Gate to the right, another tomb to another unknown soldier, another eternal flame to an anonymous boy from a small village. The four boys' heads turned from one aspect to another, as if the view from the back window of a taxi made their city new.

As we reached Lodi Gardens the heat was beginning to fade, the sunlight slipping down around the tombs of the Lodi rulers. Even so it was still too hot for the garden's usual visitors, the walkers and joggers of air-conditioned Delhi. The sparse lawns and the monuments of Lodi seemed to be ours. The children followed me to Muhammad Shah's tomb, the largest and most central, its arches of black shadow fanned by the wings of pigeons and bats.

There was a steep stairway that led up to a flat roof above the dark shadows. The boys were happy to scramble up when it was suggested, but the little girl was not so keen. She elected to wait at the bottom of the stairs, watching over the various grubby sweatshirts that I had just coaxed off her brothers. The middle-sized brother had been sporting a purple number that would have been fine but for the announcement of Michael Jackson's world tour emblazoned across the back, with a frightening picture of the pale, diminutive star, pop-eyed and ringleted, on the front. He was immensely proud of his sweatshirt but I knew it wouldn't do much for the shawls. To get him to take it off I had to ask them all to do the same. So little sister took charge of the pile and my handbag while the boys wrapped themselves in the shawls that I offered before clambering up to the roof, embarrassed by being partially disrobed and restyled in hot pashmina in the motionless air. They stood paralysed, the shawls draped around their shoulders, limp and lifeless.

By now a small crowd of the first of the afternoon walkers had gathered below us. Little sister shooed away those who tried to breach her front line in a bid for the stairs. The growing crowd made the boys feel even more self-conscious. They remained static, rigid expressions on their faces.

A fat man in a virulent green tracksuit broke past little sister in spite of her remonstrations. He was not the type to be put off by a vociferous, tousle-haired six-year-old brandishing Michael Jackson in his face. By the time he had squeezed himself to the top of the stairs he was puffing badly: his tracksuit was obviously for comfort rather than the sweat of the track. He did not look out over the tomb. He did not take in the wide view of the garden in the fading light. He did not even look down on the crowd below. He just placed himself between the boys, the camera and me, and remained there, perched uncomfortably on the edge of the roof.

A breath of air came up through the tomb and fluttered the shawls. The boys began to play, lifting the shawls and flying them over their heads, coral, lilac, pale turquoise and old rose in full flight. They danced around with their banners, sometimes bumping into the round man in his under-exercised tracksuit. He stood his ground.

I smiled at him and waved the camera about just in case he had missed the fact that I was trying to photograph the boys. He ignored me.

'*Maf kijiye* – excuse me,' I said.

'I am speaking English,' he bridled.

'Wonderful, I am so glad. But would you mind moving a little? I am trying to take some pictures.'

He looked at me, unmoved and unmoving.

Behind him the boys flew the shawls, jumping about and mimicking the round man, thrusting out their hollow stomachs at each other and puffing their thin cheeks. The shawls were bright, the sky was blue, the boys were laughing, the stone roof was rich with light.

'Please, could you move? The light is perfect. Please,' I begged.

'You are taking my photograph.' It was a statement, not a request. He smiled and tilted his head a little.

I started to photograph, the lens pointed directly at our fat friend, shutter after shutter. His smile spread and grew. He had achieved his aim.

'Lovely, thank you so much, these will be wonderful pictures.' I smiled encouragingly.

'Photo to me?'

'Of course,' I replied.

'You are taking my address. You are having paper?'

'Yes, of course. Tell me your address and I will write it down when I have taken these pictures.'

'No, no, must be writing now.'

'Right.' I had no paper or pen, and behind him the shawls were aloft in the golden light.

He called to the crowd below. A man with sad dog eyes and broken sandals made his way around little sister on the bottom step and joined us on the roof, a scrap of paper and a

The photo-session begins

pencil stub in his hand. Our tracksuit model dictated his
address letter by letter to his appointed scribe. The scrap of
paper was handed to me proudly and the sad-eyed scribe
looked at me, his dogged expression edged with hope. My
handbag was with little sister. I called to her but she refused
to move. Her brothers joined the cry. She made a grand

performance of bundling up their sweatshirts and hoisting them on to her head with my bag.

Rupees were given to the sad scribe, and the scrap of paper was safely stored in my wallet. At last our fat friend seemed satisfied. He retreated gingerly back towards the steps. There had been no film in the camera. I had been about to change the roll when he had made his stand.

Still the boys played, the breeze blew and I loaded a new film. I did not stop until the boys began to get bored, dropping the shawls and treading rather too often on my investment. We went back down to find little sister squatting over her sweatshirt pile like a nesting bird.

'Can I buy you all an ice-cream?' I asked. An ice-cream seller had appeared from the shadows and stood ready for business under his tatty umbrella.

'No thank you,' said the eldest of the boys.

I wanted to give them something, an acknowledgement of their help. Money would not have been suitable.

'What about some *bhel puri*?' The popular puffed rice, chopped onion, coriander and *masala* seemed a better idea, and a snack man had also materialized from behind a bed of Canna lilies, his little mounds of ingredients already laid out in front of him on a tray, high up on a spindly cross-legged stand. They all looked at the tray but still they would not accept.

'I would like to buy you some *bhel puri*,' I tried again.

'We are not wanting charity,' said the eldest brother.

Little sister was gazing hungrily at the *bhel puri*.

'This is not charity. You have done something for me, you have helped me, and I would like to buy you a small thing to thank you for that.'

'Then you must come to our house,' the eldest boy said.

I did not understand the link between *bhel puri* and their home.

'If you buy us this, we would like you to come to our house in return,' he explained.

It seemed a curious trade but a trade it was. The eldest brother then decided on behalf of his siblings that ice-cream was actually what they all wanted. He would not, however, choose the flavours. I had to do that, three chocolate and three vanilla, another mistake. The first three boys took the chocolate ones, leaving the smallest brother, little sister and me with second-best vanilla.

Our taxi-driver made us stand on the street and finish them before he would let us back into the car for the return journey. When we got to the road at the edge of the slum he wanted us to get out and walk the rest of the way through the pot-holes. The boys chanted in unison until he agreed to drive us to the door. He turned to me and smiled. He knew what an impression it would make, a taxi drawing up outside a slum house. But when we got there, there was no one around to be impressed. Little sister looked particularly disappointed and she slammed the taxi door with all the strength of her six years.

The children's home was beside an open *nala* full of grey sludge. The smell was choking. We arrived in the twilight. The house seemed to be empty. There was a pile of rusting soft-drink cans by the door. The eldest boy proudly pointed them out as his booty. He was paid one rupee for six kilos of cans, just over a penny. At weekends, when people picnicked in all the gardens, he said that he could collect six kilos in about three or four hours.

The house was not so much a house as a room with a roof. There was a pile of blankets in one corner next to a stack of nine bed-rolls. I still had about half of the family to meet.

'Father, Pitājī, will be coming back from the factory soon. Sit,' commanded the eldest boy.

We sat, the five of them on the floor, me on a bedroll that had been pulled out. Two more children appeared, a girl and a boy, younger than the other five. They sat down as well and watched me as I looked around the room. The girl had a bony kitten in her arms, its head blown out of proportion to its body by starvation. She pulled at its ears and tail but it did not have the energy to escape.

In spite of the number of people who obviously lived in the room it was still dank and raw, just breeze-block walls and a concrete floor. A fat Ganesha looked down from a poster, the elephant god's four chubby arms waving merrily. The poster was the only source of colour in the room, the mewing of the kitten the only sound. We waited for the arrival of Pitājī, as the twilight thickened. When he came the room rallied. The eldest boy brought in a lamp so that his father could inspect the visitor. And he did, from top to toe, while his seven assembled children looked on.

No wife appeared though Pitājī shouted for *chai* and there was a muted response from the shadows outside the room. No one in the room made reference to her, and her presence was only felt through the order for tea.

Pitājī was from Bihar and he did not understand my weak Hindustani. The second son acted as interpreter. Pitājī wanted to know why I had photographed his children. I started to explain but he did not seem to be listening. He was much more interested in looking at a dark patch on the wall close to the second of Ganesha's left hands, the one holding a lotus flower. My explanation trailed off. We sat in silence waiting for the *chai* that did not appear. After more silence, interrupted only by the mewling of the kitten, Pitājī turned his attention to me again.

'My cousin brother is living in Reading in south of UK. Are you knowing him?'

'What is his name?'

'Ram Yadav.'

'I don't think I do know him.'

Pitājī looked surprised. 'But UK is small place. You must be knowing most of people,' he persisted.

'You are absolutely right, it is a small place but I do not go to

Reading often.' I hoped this would satisfy him but he still looked disappointed, reason enough for another protracted silence.

Release came with the arrival of the tea in small glasses that were too hot to hold. We sat jiggling them from one hand to the other. I spilt most of mine on to the floor and into my lap. They all stared.

'Good *chai*?' asked Pitãjĩ, as I rubbed it into my thighs.

'Yes, very good, thank you.'

He remained straight-faced and the silence returned.

'Are you knowing any politicians?' he asked after some thought.

I hesitated, at a loss for an answer.

'Are you knowing Margaret Thatcher?' he pressed.

I had to admit I didn't.

'This is pity,' he concluded.

There was no polite way to leave their home. The best that could be done was to leave having caused the minimum of offence. I made an excuse about my landlady being concerned if I stayed out after dark unaccompanied. That was acceptable.

'You will be writing now that you are good friend to us,' Pitãjĩ stated through his interpreter.

'Yes, of course, I'm going to send copies of the pictures that I have taken today of your sons in Lodi Gardens.'

It took a long time for Pitãjĩ to find a pen and a piece of paper, even longer for him to write down the address. He was almost as slow as the sad-eyed scribe in Lodi Gardens, and when he had finished I could not read it. He had written in Bihari. I was about to say something but stopped.

'You are sure you are writing?'

I brandished the piece of paper, smiled and tried to remember if I knew any Bihari speakers.

'Of course I will.'

I left the house without having seen the children's mother. The eldest and second brothers accompanied me. As soon as we were out of sight of their home, the elder boy took a pen from his pocket and rewrote the address his father had written. He wrote in neat, clear English and gave it back to me without saying anything.

They walked me to the edge of the slum, to where the sealed road took over from the pocked dust-track that led to the breeze-block houses. There was one rickshaw in the distance. It lolled just off the road and in the dying light it was hard to tell whether it had been abandoned or merely parked at a drunken angle. As we approached we could see a *sirdar*, a Sikh, asleep in the front. His head was slumped back, showing where his beard had been carefully rolled and tucked up into the sides of his turban.

The elder boy woke the Sikh, pushing him hard enough to topple him to one side. The man was not pleased to find that his waker was a slip of a boy. No, he had no interest in taking anyone to Connaught Place in central Delhi. No, he was not concerned about the plight of an unprotected woman alone in a dark area of the city on a Saturday night. No, he did not wish to take orders from a lippy boy. Yes, if Madamjī was happy to pay double he would take her wherever she pleased.

The elder boy was angry that I had cut in at the end of his negotiations with a cheap cash incentive. When his younger brother took my hand to say goodbye the older boy turned away. I had offended the first edges of his manhood. He walked off without turning back. As the rickshaw pulled out, his younger brother stood in the middle of the road and waved. He was still waving as I lost sight of him.

I often take out the photographs from that afternoon in Lodi Gardens and look at them again because they mark the beginning. The contact sheets tell the story exactly as it happened. The early frames show the boys stiff and uncomfortable, looking at their feet and at each other. Then there is the change in mood after the round man in the redundant tracksuit made them laugh and start to play. These are the ones that I picked from the sheet and had blown up to send to my friend Robin in his leafy vicarage in Nottinghamshire; Robin, who had been in the wool trade for more than forty years but who, at that juncture, had about as much knowledge of pashmina as the rounded man in the tracksuit had of the subtleties of fashion photography. He was sitting in his pretty home, oblivious to the pictures that were on their way to him and musing on a peaceful semi-retirement, the late afternoon of his life mapped as a gently rolling landscape stretching away before him, dotted with fine food, good art, low-flying game and all manner of Epicurean delights. For a man looking out on a view of such pleasures he received the package from India with a great deal more enthusiasm than I would have summoned if our roles had been reversed. I rang him a couple of weeks after I had sent the photographs to gauge his reaction.

In Delhi it was early evening at the local telephone booth. Two cows were eating from the vegetable-seller's pile of rotting apples, oblivious to the screams of the stall's owner. A man lay on the pavement just outside the booth, his eyes closed, his limbs jutting at cruel angles. A German boy with sunburn and a white-blond ponytail was screaming at his mother on the long-distance line. It seemed to be an argument about kettles and donkeys. A tall, dark South Indian was on the local line discussing the price of plastic zips. The rest of us waited, enjoying the cross-fertilization of the conversations. My turn came after the German. In Nottinghamshire it was Sunday after church.

'Robin, hello. Did you get my package?'

'Hello, what a nice surprise. Yes, lovely. We're having a lunch party. Can we talk later?'

I looked back at the long queue stretching beyond the telephone booth and at the faces lined up on the bench, watching me.

'Not really. I'm in a telephone booth and there is a long queue.'

'Well, hang on a minute. Let me think. I rather had my mind on lunch.'

'I asked what you thought of the photographs that I sent you.'

A large Sikh was purposefully edging towards the booth.

'Yes, lovely, what do you want me to do with them?' Robin asked.

'What do you think?'

'What I am supposed to think?'

'Pashmina is going to be the next big thing that all your grand county friends will be rushing out to buy.'

'What, do you mean those shawls on the funny boys?'

'Exactly.'

'Well, I'll ask some of the girls and see what they think. Now, how do you spell it? Pash what?'

I spelt it out for him as the large Sikh hovered outside the door of the booth.

'Okay, bye.' Robin crashed the telephone down but it missed the cradle. I could hear him shouting orders about lunch and home-made raspberry ice-cream in the deep freeze while the Sikh rattled the handle of the door, waving his hand at me to hurry.

As I paid, everything suddenly went dark. Yet another of Delhi's powercuts had begun. The shops in the little bazaar soon flickered back into focus as candles were lit, and the shopkeepers and their customers were thrown into trembling silhouette. I tripped over the man lying on the pavement outside the telephone booth. He made no sound.

Robin's fuller response to the photographs came the following day. He sent a fax. He had given the matter some thought.

> Sunday p.m.
> The Old Vicarage
> Do you propose we set up some sort of business? If so, how would we sell? Mail order? Direct selling? Through shops? Are you aware of the following?

He then trailed through the salient points of setting up a business: the structure, the financing, VAT, company tax, turnover forecasts, profit and loss, each point tempered with a slight note of despondency. Only the end was encouraging.

> In principle and in spite of the above said, it does sound like rather a good idea. What does that make me now – 25% retired, 75% shawl-flogger?

> Love Robin

I went home and took out the four shawls again. They were marked from the afternoon in Lodi Gardens, and one of them had a small tear in the corner. I draped the shawl the colour of dying roses over the back of a chair and sat looking at it by candlelight. It was exquisite. A trace of the boys' smell of spice and dust still clung to it.

I sat down at my desk to write a reply to Robin.

> Dear Robin
>   You will be a very unusual kind of shawl-flogger . . .

CHAPTER 2

Mrs Clinton's Carpetman

THE INFINITE POSSIBILITIES of the shawl were made clear to me in a moment of rare public display. One Sunday afternoon, walking in a dusty Delhi municipal garden, I strolled past a young couple lying under a tree, vaguely aware that they were involved in something that was both immoral and illegal by Delhi police standards. They were conducting their afternoon's entertainment within the folds of a shawl, their activity betrayed only by the rhythmic ripple of the weave.

Robin found it harder to grasp the nature of the goods. Another fax arrived from the Old Vicarage.

> What exactly is pashmina? No one really seems to know. Apparently they murder some poor old goats to get it and it is illegal. Is this true? If so, we may be in trouble. You have to fill me in on all this. I don't know what to tell people.

Goats are not murdered, nor is pashmina illegal. *Pashan,* or *pashm,* is a Persian word meaning 'extraordinarily fine wool'. From the time when Mogul artisans first began to spin the yarn for their ruling masters in the late fifteenth century, the fine undercoat of the high-altitude goats of Ladakh has been called the *pashm.*

Traders carried shawls woven from *pashm* to the European courts. They were a great favourite among the tsarinas and tsarevnas of Russia as an exquisite solution to the iciness of their winter palaces. The Empress Josephine insisted on having one in every shade of the spectrum. When the ladies of another empire began to take to the Himalayan foothills during the hot season in the mid-nineteenth century, they noticed the floating cashmere shawls worn by the local Rajahs to keep out the evening chill.

Rather than keeping the secret of cashmere wool to themselves, the Kashmiris gave the European ladies what they wanted and set about creating something even finer for themselves and their daughters' dowries. The goatherds took their flocks higher into the mountains to graze, and the inner *pashm* grew finer still to keep out the cold. The finest of all, called pashmina, comes from the *Capra hircus*, a Himalayan goat that hops among the high crags, living on a rarefied and spartan diet. This angel hair comes especially from two places, the throat and the belly. In its perfect form it has a width of ten microns, one micron being one-millionth of a metre. Human hair is more than six times as thick.

So the goat is neither murdered nor maimed but combed through. It is not a particularly cruel practice nor is it that kind. The combs that are used would be familiar to anyone who has ever had to go through the lice-combing ordeal. It cannot be a pleasurable experience for the goat, but it is probably better to be a *Capra hircus* confronted by a fine-toothed comb than a *chiru* at the end of a hunter's gun-sights.

The *chiru* is the spring-loaded antelope that was once a familiar sight in the Hindu Kush and on the Tibetan plateau. It has the same qualities as a gazelle, its agility suspending it in the air as it leaps from hummock to tussock. When it has the advantage of a high ledge it will look down on a stranger with the black-lashed, liquid-brown eyes of a hunted Asian beauty. The *pashm* of the *chiru* is so fine it measures just five microns, twice as fine as the best pashmina. The *chiru* is also a very shy animal. Efforts to breed it in

The cashmere goats of Kashmir, and a sheep

captivity have so far failed because it has proved impossible to replicate the harshness and altitude of its natural environment in a zoo. It is stalked and shot for its fleece. One *chiru* produces about eight ounces of fleece that can be spun. The yarn of the *chiru* is woven into *shahtoosh*. The name means 'emperor of shawls' or 'cloth of kings', depending on the translation from the Persian. It takes the *pashm* of four to six *chiru* to make one shawl. *Shahtoosh* has been an important constituent of royal dowries in Asia since the *chiru* was first killed for its fleece. The value of a *shahtoosh* has always been high. The *chiru* is now a protected animal and the sale of *shahtoosh* is illegal in almost all parts of the world. As a result, the black-market price of a shawl has leapt. The dowries of the daughters of the new industrial and celluloid emperors of India still come with a few *shahtoosh*, and the gun-running guerrillas of Kashmir carry four things as collateral – heroin, guns, star rubies and *shahtoosh*.

The lure of the illegal has also tempted the rich in the West. They purse their lips over the $2,000 price tag, but then they feel the shawl and, like junkies, they spread their cash on top of the battered plastic suitcase from which the nervous dealer has just pulled his wares. They buy not just a shawl but also the frisson of owning something illegal, the expensive smell of fear.

In the same way as some confuse pashmina and *shahtoosh*, there is also confusion over the term ring-shawl, the colloquial name for *shahtoosh*.

A few weeks after my first visit in July, I returned to Abdullah the storyteller to buy more shawls to send to Robin as samples. The pavement magazine-seller gave me a wide grin and waved another copy of *Vogue* at me. It was the same edition that I had already bought from him. The spice merchant was watching from his perch on a hessian sack, his hand to his orange-lentil beard. He waved to me.

'Not to be buying more. He is asking too much of money. If you are wanting more of magazine, you are asking me and I am making good price with him for you.'

'Thank you, that is very kind.'

'Come, are you needing spices?'

The magazine-seller grumbled as I stepped into the spice shop, in amongst the sacks of cloves, cinnamon bark, cardamom, black pepper and the full spectrum of lentils. The spice merchant saw me looking at the orange ones.

'*Dhal*, you are wanting for *dhal?*' he asked, holding a handful of the lentils up and letting them fall through his fingers in a stream of colour.

I laughed. They were an exact match for his beard. He understood and stroked his dyed hair proudly.

'I have been for *haj*.'

He had made the pilgrimage to Mecca, the greatest achievement for a Muslim, and he had dyed his hair and beard as a sign that he was now a *hajji*, a veteran of Mecca.

I bought a quarter of a pound of cardamom from him, smiled apologetically at the magazine-seller and stepped around him and into Abdullah's shop.

My first question was about *shatoosh*. Abdullah produced one even before I had finished asking.

'Ah, ring-shawl. You are wanting the best. This is fabulous, incredible.'

From a pile of shawls he produced a small bundle the colour of a brown mouse. It did not have the lustre of pashmina woven with silk, the mix of the four shawls that I had bought before. In fact it looked dull. But then he put it in my hands and it slid through them. Laughing, he threw it up into the air. It floated down as if held by currents that were not there. I reached up to it like a child. It rippled around my arms. How easy it would be to hook the rich junkies.

'You know that these are illegal now, don't you?'

Abdullah put his head in his hands.

'Why, why, I am asking you, why all this drama drama?' He shook his head and threw his hands in the air.

'Because we are told that the antelopes are killed to get their fleece.'

He looked up and his blue eyes narrowed.

'So, who is so great as Allah to decide what is most important, antelope or people, my people?'

I did not understand what he meant.

'My people, whole villages in Kashmir. My people who weave *shahtoosh*. They are weaving, their fathers were weaving, and the fathers of those fathers. Now they have no food, no money to buy, nothing to burn for keeping warm. Last winter, we were having terrible weather and so many of people were dying. Why, why?'

I sat in silence.

'Because someone in his nice big warm house with his very many servants and cars is deciding he can be Allah and say no more '*toosh*. Bah, no more life for my people. I am asking you. Is this a right thing to choose antelope above my people?'

I looked down.

'Now see this.' His tone changed, his passion vented. 'See.'

It was another brown mouse. It slid through my hands in the same way, a spider's web, as fine as a wedding veil.

'Now your ring,' he demanded.

I gave him the small ring from the third finger of my right hand. The storyteller became the circus performer. He stood up and cleared his throat with grand percussion, and then he whipped the first brown mouse through the ring. A shawl woven from hair about a five-thousandth of an inch in diameter fairly flies through a narrow ring.

The Kashmiri made further throaty sounds and pulled the second brown mouse through the ring. It slipped straight through.

'See, we are having two ring-shawls. First one I am showing is *shahtoosh*. What are you thinking about second one?'

He let it slide against my cheek.

'*Shahtoosh* again?' I asked.

'Feel it, touch it.'

He bundled the second brown mouse into my hands. I did not know what I was supposed to be looking for. I studied it. The delicate threads were perhaps a little more loosely woven than those in the first shawl. He took it back.

'Both ring-shawls. You have seen with your own eyes. Incredible, no?'

He performed the trick again.

'Number one 'toosh costing a lakh, that is 100,000 rupees, very much money. Number two, tip-top one hundred per cent pashmina, the finest from Kashmir, only 10,000 rupees, incredible, a tenth of 'toosh. See how I am so happy to be biting off my own foot to do business with you, *inshallah*.'*

'*Inshallah*.' It seemed to be the best reply. But that was before an incident with a teapot.

Indian women have a way of wearing shawls. It is in their nature, their dressing-room version of falling off a log. They do not have to learn. It is an inextricable part of their femininity. Western women have somehow lost the knack. Abdullah felt that I needed to be taught how to wear a shawl. Ten years of wearing them around India was apparently not pupillage enough.

'Dear madam,' he insisted, 'you have so *very* much to learn.'

Still flushed with the excitement of the trick of the ring-shawls, he took the rose-coloured shawl from around my shoulders where it had been hanging, limp in the heat.

'You see, it is like this.'

He whirled it around his head. One end settled on his left shoulder, the majority of the shawl still flying free across his right arm. With an upward flick he looped the free end across his chest in soft folds, instantly softening the grey of his *feron*. Then he admired himself in the shop mirror, resettling the long end across his chest again so that it fell even more elegantly.

'Now you are doing.'

* 100,000 rupees is roughly £1,450.

He pulled another shawl from his pile. It was the colour of plane-tree leaves when the wind blows and catches the silvery undersides in the sunlight.

'Try again, my dear. You will also be taking Kashmiri tea.' His statement meant that it was time to sit down and discuss finance.

He shouted up the stairs for tea. There was silence in the room above, followed by the pad of bare feet stirred into action.

Abdullah opened the negotiations with a price far higher than I had paid for the first four shawls. He had sensed my excitement, my eagerness to buy.

One of the boys came quietly down the stairs with a tray and started to pour the tea. Abdullah whisked shawls in and out of plastic bags, sliding them through my fingers: burning pink, the red of pure saffron and flame orange, the colours of Rajasthani women in the evening light on sunbaked roads; cream, camel and dark butter, the shades of melting sugar as it simmers from fudge to toffee; lichen silvered on an ash tree, English lawn green, the voluptuous brown of field mushroom underbelly after rain. But he never gave me enough time to study the feel of them, to compare the sheen of the silk from one to another or to check the ply or the delicate hatching of the warp and weft.

The boy pouring the tea seemed nervous and splashed some on one of the shawls. Abdullah howled and lashed out. The boy, the tea, the pot and the cup flew, landing on a blood-red shawl. The boy whimpered, the spout broke off the teapot and the cup rolled, but the tea sat in a perfectly contained island on the surface of the shawl.

Two things had been proved beyond reasonable doubt: pashmina woven with silk was hot-shower proof and, of more importance to the immediate future, Abdullah had a streak of cruelty, a lack of control. I was not sure I really wanted to do business with him. Even so, I knew that if I bought nothing, the tea-pourer would suffer. I selected two shawls from the pile that had managed to escape the shower of tea: one the colour of the thick crust on top of unpasteurized Jersey cream, the other a washed mauve, the colour of fading blue hydrangeas.

There was no rent money left to hand over. I gave Abdullah a credit card instead. There was a problem with the Central Reserve Bank of India and the credit-card police who alight on random transactions and turn them into an inquisition. Abdullah passed the telephone to me.

'Date of birth?' barked the credit-card policeman. 'Mother's maiden name?'

She had more than one as a result of her mother having married several times. I could not remember which one I had given the bank for security clearance sixteen years before.

'Mother's maiden name?' he demanded again.

I eventually got it right but had to wait another ten minutes before being given authorization. The holding music was a digitally pulverized version of 'You've Got a Friend' by my school dormitory-wall hero, James Taylor. I did not have a friend.

'You will of course be coming back to me, *inshallah*,' Abdullah announced.

'*Inshallah*,' I replied weakly.

A large American, one hand resting nervously on his money pouch, the other mopping a very sweaty forehead, came into the shop as I bundled the two new shawls into my bag.

'Most wonderful evening to you, sir.' Abdullah bowed.

The man looked around the piled shelves.

'I guess I'm looking for a shawl for ma wife. She's not too well right now.'

'Sit, sit, please,' Abdullah cajoled. 'Your wife, what colour is her liking?'

'Well, she's kinda fussy,' said the American, as he tried to find a way of sitting down on the carpet from Srinagar. His stomach and money belt made it difficult.

'Let me show you things,' Abdullah said.

He called to the boys upstairs to bring down the calico bundles and passed the American some from the pile that he had been selling to me.

'Just tell me which one says "hello" to you.'

A new customer, new banter.

'It is perhaps time for your wife to have pashmina.'

'What's that?' asked the trapped tourist.

'Ah, let me tell you a story.'

A new customer, the same old banter.

The storyteller did not acknowledge my departure.

I had just two more shawls to send to Robin. He would need more than that to start a business. He was begging me for samples and I had just severed my first tentative relationship with a supplier because of spilt tea. I needed to buy pashmina but now I had no source. Yet I knew that up in Kashmir the weavers were sitting in their villages, the shuttles of their looms flying back and forth in the half-lit rooms of their wooden houses, weaving late into the evening as the light died away through their windows, falling off the mountains, sending shards of light the colour of crushed cranberries and sun-bleached lavender across the lakes of Srinagar, setting alight the reflection of the willow trees on the water, then fading away so fast that the weavers were forced to press their faces right up to the weft on the loom to make sure that their shuttles flew straight. They can only weave by daylight. The electricity is infrequent, and trembling when it comes, playing games with the delicate meeting of the weft and the warp. While I sat in Delhi without a source the weavers were trying to find ways of working around the privations of living in a tinderbox zone that had once grown fat on the tourist dollar. While India and Pakistan spat at each other over the disputed lakes, meadows and willow trees of the Kashmir valley, the weavers wanted to be able to eat, to keep their children in school, to observe their fasts and celebrate their festivals without the shadow of international terrorism lengthening through their wooden casements.

The city, the valley and the Kashmiri Himalaya mark the cultural boundary of Islam. The people of the valley had once believed their rulers to be the personifications of divine power – the great temples of the eighth and ninth centuries along the Jhelum river outside Srinagar were built to commemorate them. They had also worshipped the Nagas. These creatures, half-man, half-serpent, had once lived beneath the water that had originally covered the whole of the valley floor. As the vast lake of Kashmir began to shrink the people believed that the Nagas slithered up to the higher mountain lakes and rivers, their strength increased by the rarer air of the peaks.

Islam came to the valley in the fourteenth century with the arrival of a large number of followers of the noted Persian Muslim ruler, Shah Hamdan. With the new religion came new skills – carpet-making and weaving, embroidery and papier mâché.

By the time the fourth Mogul emperor, Jahangir, lay on his deathbed in 1627, the valley had become a great prize. To generations of invaders entering India through the bleak passes of the surrounding mountains the Vale of Kashmir was a dream of water and willow trees, palely beautiful women and apple blossom. When asked if there was anything else he desired, Jahangir replied, 'Only Kashmir,' and breathed his last.

The British, like their invading predecessors the Moguls, lusted after the fertile valley. However, the princes of Kashmir never let them acquire land or build in their state. So, with the ingenuity of those driven to the edge of madness by the heat of the plains, the men of Empire came up with the idea of building miniature English country houses that could float among the lilies of Dal and Nagin Lakes. They got the idea from an enterprising shopkeeper called Pandit Narandais. When his shop was burnt down in the city, he simply transferred his wares on to a barge and continued to ply his trade; and to counter the mountain chill at night he put up a room on the barge, and so the houseboat business began.

When the subcontinent was partitioned in 1947, Hari Singh, the Maharaja of Kashmir, sought autonomy for his state. He appeared to be in a strong position. His fertile valley state lay astride the line that Jinnah intended to take for West Pakistan and that Nehru wanted for independent India. The Maharaja believed he was in a position to trade one side off against the other.

As it turned out, things were not quite so simple. The Maharaja of Kashmir was a Dogra, a Hindu whose forebears had signed a treaty with the British whereby their royal family was recognized as the ruling dynasty of Jammu and Kashmir in exchange for substantial payments into the imperial coffers. But the majority of the Maharaja's subjects were Muslim. While the rest of India rallied against the British under the banner of 'Quit India', the Kashmiri Muslims had their own cry of 'Quit Kashmir', directed at their Hindu ruler.

Hari Singh's bluff was called when in October 1947 Pathan insurgents from Baltistan invaded the valley from the north in a bid to claim Kashmir for the new nation of Pakistan. As they closed on the Kashmiri capital of Srinagar the Maharaja opted to join India and then fled to Jammu, the winter capital of his state. The Indian Army arrived to repel the invasion and so began the first Indo-Pakistan war. The conflict continued until 1948 when the United Nations imposed a cease-fire. Kashmir was left divided along the line where the fighting had stopped. Again in 1965 Pakistan tried but failed to seize the state. Since then Kashmir has continued to fester like an open sore. Continual political tension has made extremists of many hitherto moderate Kashmiris. Militancy has grown, as have separatist demands, and the death toll has continued to mount.

Somehow I had to try and find another Kashmiri pashmina supplier to bring me the work from the weavers of the troubled state, but I did not know where to look. I had found Abdullah only by chance. I walked away from Jor Bagh market without any particular direction in mind, concentrating on the problem of where to go in search of shawls. I was barely aware of the traffic honking and screaming as I crossed and re-crossed the road. What I did know was that I was too hot. My clothes clung to me and my face throbbed. Sweat ran down my arms and off the ends of my fingers. It was now August and the temperature was somewhere in the region of 40°C. As I hailed a rickshaw I could see the driver laughing at me. I got in, too hot even to attempt to be graceful.

'Where to?' asked the driver.

I named the nearest five-star hotel where there were cool, high ceilings, marble corridors, bathrooms with endless supplies of soft loo paper and attendants proffering towels, and a coffee shop serving tall fresh lime sodas, the icy condensation running down the outside of the glass.

'*Which* place?' asked the driver incredulously. My damp, crumpled appearance did not, in his mind, accord with five-star hotels.

I repeated the name of the hotel. He shrugged and kicked his rickshaw into motion, swerving out into the flow of angry traffic. He deposited me at the bottom of the grand driveway that sweeps up from the road to the front of the hotel. He charged me twice the normal fare for the distance covered. There was not much room for argument over a few rupees when he was dropping me at a hotel with a nightly room tariff equivalent to his annual earnings.

I stopped in the doorway to enjoy the first rush of air-conditioning as it turned the sweat cold on my prickling skin. And then my answer came out of a crowd of Japanese tourists in the lobby.

They were neat, chattering, uniformed in designer logos and criss-crossed with Nikon camera straps. Threading his way through them with a pile of rolled carpets balanced across his arms came a Kashmiri. His nose was sculpted in the same way as Abdullah's and it was just resting on top of the carpets. He peered at the ground in front of him with eyes the colour of the *chiru*, melting brown. He moved silently, tripping over the hem of his *feron* that had been pulled down by his load. He was younger than Abdullah but otherwise physically quite similar. One sweet difference seemed apparent: even as he tripped on his hem, struggling to keep his carpets aloft, he was silent. There was no show of impatience, no irritation. I thought I even saw him smile when one of his stumbles nearly brought him down.

He made his way across the hall of the grand hotel and away from the crowd of Japanese. He stopped next to one of the cool marble pillars, carefully unloaded his carpets, straightened his *topi*, the skull cap on the back of his thick black hair, and re-adjusted his *feron*. He examined the throng around him in the hall and then looked back to his pile of carpets on the floor. Having made another slow study of the crowd he set off at an upright jog down a corridor leading from the hall. His head turned constantly to check his unguarded carpets. And each time he looked he tripped over his hem.

He returned almost immediately, trailed by a younger man whose beard had the wispiness of adolescence. The first man was probably in his late thirties, the younger man perhaps twenty. The carpets were stacked on to the arms of the younger man and he was chivvied off down the corridor. But there seemed to be no aggression in the way the older man hurried the boy along. He gave him orders but it was gently done. His eyes looked too wide and open for there to be venom in his lowered tone. I followed them down the corridor.

We crossed into a shopping arcade, past half a dozen jewellery shops with their interchangeable *bijouterie*, past the Mont Blanc concession where the assistants wore sharp black suits and smiles to match. Next to a stationer's selling coffee-table books of the Taj Mahal from dawn till dusk, the Kashmiri, the carpets and the boy turned into a shop. Above the entrance a sign read:

National Cottage Emporium
Prop. **Wangnoo Bros.** Headquartered. **Srinagar.**
Purveyors of all finest of **Kashmir**

In the corner of one of the windows was a pile of shawls, possibly, probably, pashmina shawls. As I hovered outside, three front-of-house boys from other shops slunk over, entreating me to see their shops. One proffered papier mâché, the second carpets 'absolute guarantee one hundred per cent silk', the third all manner of jewels. But no one came out of the National Cottage Emporium.

It seemed to be quiet inside the shop when I entered. The room was empty and only partially lit by a narrow window half-way up a staircase that led up and out of the shop. But as the shadows adjusted I realized that I was wrong. There was someone else in the room. He was sitting in the corner, cross-legged and quiet on a small carpet, its fringed edges just appearing beneath the hem of his *feron*. His eyes were closed and his lips moved silently.

People usually leave when they find someone at prayer. I did not. Instead, hoping that I had come into the pale light quietly enough not to have been noticed, I sat down in another corner and waited for him to finish.

A telephone cracked the silence but the Kashmiri did not stir. The telephone continued to ring. The younger boy who had carried the carpets back to the shop appeared from the stairs and answered the call. There followed a loud conversation in excited Kashmiri.

The praying man remained motionless except for his constantly moving lips. The telephone call ended. The boy banged down the receiver and went back upstairs. He had not seen me in the dim corner. Again there was silence.

The man at prayer opened his eyes.

'*Salaam alekum* – good afternoon to you.' He readjusted himself on his small carpet. 'It is a great thing that you have been sitting with me for prayer. We will have good business.'

I smiled.

'Now you are telling me how I am helping you.'

'Well, yes, I hope you can.' I continued to smile.

'Of this I am having no doubt. I am Ashraf Wangnoo. We are four Wangnoo brothers from Kashmir. We are all doing business together. I am number three brother.'

'It is a pleasure to meet you. My name is Justine. I have a brother and a sister but we are not in business together.'

Ashraf laughed. 'Now I am knowing all things except what you are wanting.'

'I am trying to find pashmina.'

'Ah, all the peoples are looking for pashmina. I am having calls from US of A, from UK, all the places, all the same, have you pashmina? We are making business with Mrs Hillary Clinton, you know.'

He pointed to a framed letter above where he sat. It was from the desk of Hillary Rodham Clinton, the White House. It thanked the Wangnoo brothers for their very high quality of service. The carpets had arrived safely, as Mr Wangnoo had said they would. They looked lovely and were a great enhancement to the rooms in the White House where they had been laid. Mrs Clinton had signed herself with a flourish.

'How wonderful, and did Mrs President buy any pashmina from you?' I asked.

'No, people are telling me she is a very clever lady but I am thinking that she is not clever with her outfitting. I am surprised that she is not getting more of assistance.'

'I am sure she is but perhaps her advisers were not with her when she was in your shop.'

'This must have been what was happening. I will show you pashmina. Come, you must see some beautiful carpets too.'

He could not resist that. It was in his nature. He was a devout Muslim, but he was also a Kashmiri with a heritage of floor coverings and a godown in Delhi full of carpets. The pashmina was, after all, just a sideline. Ashraf was going to give me the full show.

He did not tell me any wild stories about birds of paradise. He went straight to the point and covered the floor with pashmina shawls in every colour from ivory to magenta. I sat in the middle, surrounded by the artistry of his valley's weavers.

'I hope you will not think this a rude question, but your name doesn't sound very Kashmiri,' I said as I fingered some of the one hundred per cent weave, fragile as butterfly wings, and the more voluptuous pashmina woven with silk, the kind that I had draped around the boys in Lodi Gardens and that I had seen on the baby from Lahore pictured in *Vogue*.

'You are so right. It is Chinese name.' Ashraf continued to pull out more shawls.

'How interesting. Where does it come from?'

'China,' he replied. 'Let me show you something.'

He jumped up and disappeared up the stairs, returning with a small carpet, perhaps only a foot square.

'You are knowing that *'toosh* is the emperor of shawls? Well, this is king emperor of carpets. See this.' He held it towards me with reverence, as if it were a religious relic. 'Look at the workmanship. It is the tree of knowledge, see, each branch being a twig of learning. Look at the knotting, unbelievable.' He turned the small square over. 'Very highest quality floor-covering carpets are having 576 knots per inch squared. This one 5,000, can you believe this? Let me show you.' He took an eye-glass and placed it on the back of the carpet.

I put my eye to it and there was an inch marked out at the base of the glass.

'Count them, count the knots – here, use this pointy pin.' He passed a long pin.

It took some time to count across the width of the marked inch. I had to restart several times when the pin came too close to the glass, blurring my vision.

Ashraf waited.

There were seventy knots across the inch and I could well believe that there were seventy rows within the inch. Even I could see that about 5,000 knots per inch was possible.

'Unbelievable.'

Ashraf smiled. 'It is more costly than buying many of finest pure pashmina shawls.'

'I will stick to the shawls for the moment.' I passed the little carpet back to him, his glass still fixed in my eye, the pin in my hand.

Ashraf retrieved both the glass and the pin and then asked, 'How much of pashmina will you be wanting to buy?'

I did not have a fixed figure in mind.

'I am buying on behalf of a business colleague, Robin Boudard. He is just starting in the pashmina line.' I set Robin in place as the masculine front of the company.

'So you will be buying much pashmina?' Ashraf lowered his voice. 'We will find you wholesale price that will be making you very happy, best prices, that is my word. Now you will come to my house in Kashmir. We have a house in Srinagar. Have you been to Kashmir?'

I told him that I had been there a few times, but not since the early 1990s when tourists were frightened away and the conflict between India and Pakistan began to escalate.

'It is a great crime what has happened in my valley. So many peoples have died. Some people are saying as many as 60,000 since 1989. That is nearly four times as much as in all three Indo-Pak wars. Too many in such a beautiful place. What to do?' Ashraf clutched the back of his neck, his fingers biting into the skin. 'Do you think my valley is very beautiful?' He waved towards a picture of a house on the wall beside the telephone, lit by the pale light from the window on the stairs.

It was typical of the houses of successful Kashmiri traders in Srinagar, a swooping roof above three storeys of bright brick and plaster, modern and sharp in comparison to the softer, balcony-layered traditional wooden Mogul houses. There were beds full of flowers in front of Ashraf's house and a willow tree.

'This is my house where you will be staying when you come to Kashmir. We are living close by to Nagin Lake. You will find that it is more than beautiful.' His hand relaxed on the back of his neck.

Nagin is the smaller of the two lakes that mingle with the city of Srinagar. In the years of Kashmir's tourist boom it had also been the quieter of the two, the perfect mirror image of its fringing poplars less frequently disturbed by the paddles of *shikaris*, the lake boatmen, than on the larger Dal Lake.

'Where have you been staying when you are in Srinagar?' asked Ashraf.

'To start with, foreign journalists coming from Delhi were auto-matically put in the Broadway Hotel. I think the authorities thought we would be easier to control if we were all in one place. It also meant that if they wanted to tell us something we were all together.'

'You were not staying at Oberoi Palace?' he pressed.

The Oberoi is the former palace of the Maharaja of Kashmir and the only hotel that Ashraf considered suitable for visitors. It was not where the government wanted journalists covering the Kashmir situation in the 1990s to be based.

'You were always staying in the one place?' Ashraf shifted his *topi* and scratched his head.

'Well, no. I then went to stay in the Hotel Pomposh. It was half way between the two rival offices of information where we had to go for permission to be allowed to step outside our hotel rooms.' I didn't tell him it was also cheaper. The newspaper that I had

The houseboats and poplars of Nagin Lake

been writing for in 1991 and 1992 hadn't run to expensive hotels.

'Hotel Pomposh is not a good place.'

'You are right.'

He was right. It had been a dank, stinking place, the cockroaches more comfortable in their surroundings than the few guests.

'Some of us then went out on to the lakes to stay on houseboats because it was much easier to get out to the villages from the lakes without being followed by the police or the military. We were seen as being disobedient troublemakers.'

'How is this? Best thing in Srinagar is to stay on houseboats. Where were you staying?'

'My landlady in Delhi recommended Mr Butt to me, on Nagin Lake. She felt that he was very trustworthy.' I paused, realizing the implication of what I had just said.

Ashraf put up his hand and stopped me as I began to apologize. 'Dear Madam, your landlady is a wise person. She is from Kashmir?'

'No, she is from Patiala.'

'Ah, it is not so far. She understands my people. I will tell you one thing for sure about my valley. We Kashmiris are not trusting any peoples but, most of all, we are not trusting each other. But Butt is a good man.'

'Do you know him?'

'But of course, everyone on Nagin is knowing everyone.'

'If I had known, I could have stayed with you.'

'All this is now corrected. Now you are knowing the Wangnoos you will always be staying with us when you are coming to Kashmir. What was the name of the houseboat you were staying on?'

I had stayed on two, first the *Princess Diana* in 1991 and then the *Princess Grace* in 1992. Mr Butt had had an obsession with blonde princesses with movie-star glamour. The third boat had been called *Queen Noor*.

'And what are your houseboats called?' I asked Ashraf.

'*Diva, Bellissima, Wuzmal* and *Michael Jackson*,' he said proudly. '*Michael Jackson* is best but we are thinking, my brothers and me, we might be changing name. He is a very famous man but we are not liking the music he is making, and I am thinking that it is not so right that a man should be such good friend with a monkey.' He looked deep into his palms.

A memory of tabloid coverage of a chimpanzee called Bubbles came to mind but I couldn't remember the nature of the connection with Michael Jackson.

'I am thinking maybe Hillary Rodham Clinton, but my brothers are saying that this is wrong and we should be calling it Bill Clinton.'

It was hard to know what to say, because I certainly did remember Monica Lewinsky and *her* connection with the President.

'Perhaps something a little less political,' I suggested tactfully. 'Your houseboat will undoubtedly last longer than his Presidency.'

'This is what I am saying to my brothers. Maybe Mrs Hillary will be first lady President of United States. Then how clever we would be to have houseboat named in her honour.'

'It could be just Hillary. Then, if she doesn't make the presidency, it will just be a boat called Hillary.'

'This is a good idea. I am telling my brother this idea of ours. Things of politics we have to be being careful. I have a friend who is fascinated by all things of politics. First he is calling his boat *The Indira*. Then he changes it to *The Benazir* and then it was *The Winnie*. But now he is tired of painting names out and putting in new ones.' Ashraf sighed.

'Sounds as if he is more interested in powerful women than politics,' I said.

Ashraf was silent. He waited for a few moments and then continued without reference to my previous comment.

'Do you not find it strange that United States are supposed to be ahead in all things, most modern country in the world, but still no lady President? India first, then Pakistan and now who knows what all else, but no United States number one lady. I am finding this most interesting.'

'The First Ladies seem resigned to writing books about the cats and kitchens of the White House,' I replied.

'Does Mrs Hillary like cats?'

'I'm not sure but I have a feeling that she does not like them very much. I think the preference in the presidential household is for dogs.' I could not remember whether it was Mrs Hillary or Mrs Cherie who harboured the greater dislike for cats in high places.

'If she is not liking cats then she is not liking Kashmiris,' he announced.

The link was unclear.

'The cat is not trusting any peoples, just like Kashmiris.'

Ashraf's feline traits started and stopped with his luxuriant whiskers. His smile was much more dog than cat.

'Now, my dear, we are talking of many things but pashmina.

I will show you all there is to know. You will come to Kashmir and see my house and my people who are making shawls for you. I will give you good price, the best price. You will take tea?'

So businesss began with the Wangnoos.

CHAPTER 3

The
Colours of Pashm

The Old Vicarage
12 September 1998

My fashionable friends tell me that the chic'est women
are fighting over pashmina. The prices they are apparently paying seem quite absurd to me. Will people
really pay £400 for an old shawl? Surely we will not be
charging anything like that? Am sending some cuttings
from the papers about pashmina. It seems to be everywhere. Have told a few people that I am about to start
selling it. Orders pouring in. When are you coming
back and how much will you be bringing with you?

Love Robin

Delhi
Still too hot
Monsoon now two months late

Found a good source – four brothers, Kashmiri Muslims
with a strange Chinese name. They are friends of
Hillary Clinton's. Is this a good or bad thing?

Sending some of the shawls and bringing more with me when I come back in November. Planning to spend some time with the dyers before I come back. Hope to do some clever things with unusual colours.

Love Justine

The dyeing shops of Delhi are a vital part of the city's fashion establishment, redyeing saris and *salwar kameez* from the bohemian colony of Nizamuddin to the more establishment residential area of Golf Links. But they do not stick to health and safety regulations as we know them. There is no Clause IV section iii stating that an employer must make every effort to preserve the lives of his employees. When Mrs Bhala wants to have her sari dyed dangerous chemical orange, a slip of a boy will reach for the can of chemical additive 776412 to fulfil her whim. He will open it and stick his hands straight into the caustic cocktail. The large skull-and-crossbones label on the can does not act as a warning. It is just part of the language of dyeing. Every can has one. They would not dye properly without it. Naked hands go in and out of the chemical pots and the dyeing vats, grabbing at pieces that have been in too long, stopping Mrs Bhala's sari from going one shade too surreal. Sweat is wiped from faces with those chemically doused hands. Most of the boys who work in the dyeing shops have skin disorders and respiratory infections of varying severity.

Ashraf gave me every assurance that he and his brothers had worked their way through all the dyers in Lajpat Nagar, the city's dyeing district. They had finally alighted on Parveen Dyers, most assuredly the finest dyers in the whole of Delhi.

Robin and I had decided to invest in some unfinished stock so that we could dye according to the seasonal shades dictated by current fashion. I had bought fifty raw shawls, each one the colour of a sheep on a hill in the rain.

Ashraf and I were sitting in the semi-darkness of his shop. There was another power-cut. Ashraf was showing me colour charts, but the grey polluted afternoon fog soaked the light away from the small window. It was impossible to try and translate the tiny boxes of colour into a six-foot length of shawl. I could imagine the powdery pink on the snippet in front of me turning into too much square footage of bad salmon mousse. In the drifting light the pinks faded into the reds, the orange into coral. Ashraf sighed.

'I am going to prayer. It is the time. You will be staying here. My number one brother Manzoor will be coming for prayer. He will be happy to meet you. He will look after all the needful when I am in Kashmir. You will like him. He is very best of man.'

'I'd be delighted to meet your brother. How long will you be at prayer?'

'Not so long.' He got up and put on his shoes.

'Are you going out to pray?'

'Yes, to mosque for giving of thanks for safe delivery at airport of brother Manzoor from Kashmir.'

'How far away is the mosque?' I asked.

'Just five minutes, just to the end of the road.'

'Ashraf, may I come to the dyers with you the next time you go?'

'We will be discussing all these things after prayer.' He waved his hand and disappeared with a shout to those upstairs. A small crew of assistants filed down and out of the shop in his wake. The mullah's call had to be answered.

I was left alone with just the sound of the money man upstairs clicking the keys on his adding-machine – a Hindu accountant playing a rhythm of his own on the calculator.

Ashraf had left his copy of the Koran beside where he had been sitting. There was a marker in one of the pages. I reached out to pick up the book but stopped before I touched it. I did not know whether Ashraf would see it as an invasion of his privacy. Would

I pick up another man's copy of the Bible or the Upanishads? I probably would. Lifting the book carefully, I opened the marked page. A short section had been underlined. I tried to copy the Arabic into my notebook. My attempt was haphazard and lacked the flow of the original but perhaps a translator would be able to tell me what it was that had moved Ashraf to underline the piece.

He had told me how much he liked to read, but the only book that I had seen was the Koran. His definition of a love of books was his great love of one book. Islam shaped every word that he uttered: every decision he made and every ambition he harboured faced towards Mecca.

As I sat in the fading light Ashraf drove his assistants to prayer, hurtling down the road, screaming at any man, woman, child or cow that crossed his path, weaving across the lanes, spinning the wheel loosely between his hands as if it were a toy, his *feron* tangling with the gear-stick – a Muslim missile, just out of control, heading for the mosque. His belief that Allah would protect him was unassailable, an ever-fixéd conviction that he would carry to the grave.

The conflict within Kashmir has erased any give-and-take among many of the valley's Muslims, leaving them with an extreme orthodoxy that shuts out many of the Western values that underpinned their economy through the 1960s, '70s and '80s.

In agreeing to do business with a foreign female unbeliever the Wangnoo brothers had already breached many of the lower-ranking codes of their religion. But this was defensible because hard foreign currency gave them the power to protect the lifestyle that furthered the cause of Allah. It meant that Manzoor, the eldest of the four brothers, could afford to send his children to school overseas, to a specialist Islamic school outside Manchester. There students spend seven years studying only the Koran until its *suras*, its verses and lessons, become second nature to them, part of the air they breathe, their food, their thought and the structure of their dreams.

It was Yaseen, the chief assistant of the Wangnoos, who took me through the early lessons of Islam. He had always worked with the brothers, but more importantly, he had always worked *for* them, as had his father. Yaseen was in his early forties, the same age as Manzoor. He had grown up beside the elder Wangnoo. He knew every dot and cross in the minutiae of the brothers' daily transactions. He had always been vital to the business, a right arm, but also always an appendage, an employee.

The strictures of Islam seemed somehow a little more relaxed around Yaseen, perhaps because he was an employee. He was no less devout than the brothers but some of the formalities were omitted. It was easier to talk to him about the areas of his religion that left me confused, even after logical explanation.

Yaseen was a slight man, his profile straight from a Mogul miniature of an artisan of the Vale of Kashmir, jagged cheekbones and a double swoop of high forehead and arching nose with a teardrop end that nestled in his moustache. His beard and hair were scattered with grey. He wore his silvering with pride, the badge of his experience.

While I waited for Ashraf, Yaseen and the others to return from prayer I tried to pair up symbols in the Arabic text that I had copied from Ashraf's Koran. Yaseen broke into my frustration.

'Good afternoon, madam.' His profile came across the page.

'Yaseen, I am so glad you have come back. I have been trying to understand something. Could you translate it for me, please?' I offered the scrawl in my notebook.

He squinted at it but made no comment about the poor copy.

'We are still having cut. No good light for reading. I am taking it to the window.'

As he crossed the room I noticed another man standing behind him. He waited silently in the doorway, watching the exchange. Yaseen twisted my notebook in the light of the window.

'I am sorry it is so badly written. I do not know how to write Arabic.'

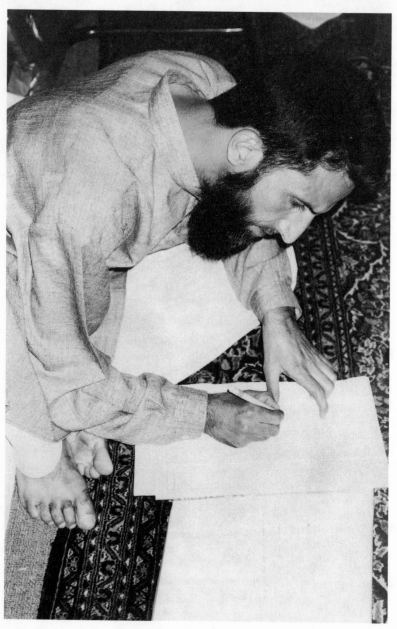

Yaseen's fine profile bent over his books

'No, madam, it is not your script, it is the fault of my sight. It is not so good now.' He peered at the paper, his nose almost touching it, and then pushed it away as if trying to focus.

'It is from the Koran,' he said.

'Yes, I copied it.' I knew I was admitting something that was not wholly acceptable.

'Some are believing that it is not right to take small snips from the Koran. It must be read as one whole piece. But for most of us all is fine. We accept all things. It is our religion.'

He walked back from the window, his mouth set, contemplating the faintly distasteful task of trying to work out my attempt at Arabic. He looked towards the man who had remained motionless beside the door. The stranger nodded.

'You have written here from the twenty-fifth *sura* – Those who are serving the Merciful One are walking softly on the earth; and when the foolish are talking to them, they are answering "Peace!"' Yaseen handed my notebook back to me.

The man in the shadows had given Yaseen licence to quote from their holy book. Now he stepped out of his silhouette in the doorway.

'*Salaam alekum*. I am Manzoor, number one of Wangnoo brothers. My third brother Ashraf has been saying much of you.' He paused, waiting for a response.

It was not clear how I should address the senior Wangnoo brother. He was a slightly older reflection of Ashraf, a little taller, a little greyer. I called Ashraf by his name as he had asked me to. I was not sure I should do the same with Manzoor. I bowed my head, my hands together in the usual formal Indian greeting.

'You are reading from our book?' he asked.

'I wish I could but I cannot read Arabic.'

'Yaseen is helping you. Soon you will be reading Koran. This is good, very good. Come, sit,' ordered Manzoor.

I sat exactly where he indicated.

It was Manzoor rather than Ashraf who gave his blessing to my proposed visit to the dyer under the guidance of Yaseen.

Even though the excesses of the hot season were beginning to fade I had to ask Yaseen to open the car window. Fear was making me sweat. He was explaining the poetry of the Koran, the use of the forces of nature as rhyme, meter and tutor. As he made each of his salient points he traversed dramatically across the lanes of traffic, apparently heedless of the cars to left and right. One of his manoeuvres was so extreme that the journey was momentarily thrown into slow motion. I saw too clearly the *kohl* eyeliner on a child leaping into the traffic as it roared blindly through a red light. There was more than enough close-up detail on the sari hem of a woman trying to hail a rickshaw.

'It is song of life, beautiful, so beautiful,' Yaseen continued. 'Going round all the time, perfect circle. You are reading Koran now?'

I was not, but I had found what I had been told was one of the great versions in translation. Yaseen was looking at me, waiting for an answer. I wanted him to look at the road.

'I have a translation,' I admitted.

He turned back to the road and was silent for a moment, drumming his fingers on the wheel.

'How much are you knowing of Islam?' he asked eventually.

'Not very much. But I like to go to Jama Masjid on Friday to see everyone coming out from evening prayer.' Jama Masjid, the most important mosque in Delhi, the biggest in India, was the final architectural flourish of Shah Jahan, completed in 1658, just a few months before his son Aurangzeb locked him up in the Octagonal Tower at Agra Fort, where he died looking out on to his other great bid for eternity, the Taj, his gift to Mumtaz, his wife for seventeen years and the mother of fourteen of his children. Jama

Masjid has two great minarets, each one over a hundred feet high, candy-striped in pink and white, sandstone and marble. The minarets drink the twilight and burn, great sticks of Brighton Rock, alight after evening prayer.

'Ah, great place, everything in there is holy, everything, all the same, more and more of poetry.' Yaseen thought again, and the car drifted across the lanes. He was away with the muezzin's call from the minaret of Jama Masjid. And then two boys, maybe eighteen or nineteen, drove past in a brand-new BMW, the windows down, a flavour-of-the-month Hindi movie soundtrack at full volume. The boy driving was paying virtually no attention to the traffic.

Yaseen looked across at him. His eyes were cold. 'All the loud music that I am hearing, all this noisy noise. This is not a good thing. It is making all the minds of the young people very much confused.'

'It is all part of being young.' I said to the window.

Yaseen heard me.

'This is not making it right. In Kashmir my children are not listening to these kinds of music, they are not watching so much of TV.'

It was the first time Yaseen had mentioned his family.

'I did not realize that you had children. How old are they?'

'Same as older ones of Manzoor. I think perhaps they are fifteen and thirteen.'

'And they really do not listen to music?'

'They are out of house doing healthful things. They are playing *kerket*.'

'Of course.' I had not heard about *kerket*. 'And they really never watch television?'

Yaseen thought.

'Yes, I remember, they have been watching TV. Manzoor had TV for news and *kerket*. For big *kerket* final my boys were going to house of Manzoor for watching. Same for soccer World Cup. But then when France was beating Brazil, Manzoor says "No more,

this is too much of rubbish. France can never have beaten Brazil."
So no more of TV.'

'They show *kerket* on television?'

'Of course.'

'I don't think I have seen it. Is it shown on one of the satellite
sports channels?' I asked.

Yaseen looked at me in astonishment. The car swerved across
the road again and a speeding freight driver sat on his horn.

'But we are having top man from your country talking about it
on TV and in papers. How can you not have been seeing this? Mr
Geoffrey Boycott from your Yorkshire pie place.'

'Pudding, Yorkshire pudding. Cricket, I've got it, cricket.'

'Of course, *kerket*.' Yaseen shook his head. 'How can you not
have been seeing this?'

'I do not watch very much television but I have seen some
coverage.'

Yaseen looked relieved. 'This is good, very great game.' Then
he turned back to the road.

'We are making small detour, I hope you are not minding this
thing. I have a very important piece to deliver on behalf of
Manzoor on way to dyer.'

Again Yaseen careered across the road and turned off the
flyover and down into one of the most exclusive residential colony
areas of Delhi, Golf Links, just next door to a keystone of the city's
establishment, the Golf Club, with its rolling greens and shade-
skirted trees.

'You must see what I am to be delivering.' Yaseen leant over into
the back seat, one hand still on the wheel, his eyes far from the road.
He put a crumpled bag on my lap. 'See, look closely at this work, it is
pashmina shawl of finest embroidery. Manzoor has been having it
repaired in Srinagar. Only one man in whole of city is having ability
for this kind of work. This piece is being over one hundred years.'

I took the shawl from the bag as we pulled up at the gates of the
colony. Yaseen leapt out of the car, *feron* and beard flying, to take

up his case with the gatekeeper who did not seem keen to allow the speeding Kashmiri in.

The shawl unfolded across my lap, falling in layers of pale grey, the embroidery so delicate, so intricate that at first I could hardly distinguish it from the weave. The fine silk of the embroiderer's thread had faded to the colours of rose petals drying on autumn lawns, old gold, ochre, deep, soft umber, the pinks of September light. It was one of the most beautiful things I had ever seen.

Yaseen came back from his altercation with the gatekeeper.

'I am thinking this man is perhaps a little of mad. He is not letting me bring car into colony. I will run quickly to house and deliver shawl.' He took the bag from me and refolded the shawl.

He seemed not to have taken offence at the refusal to permit him access. In fact he smiled at the gatekeeper as the gate was grudgingly opened just wide enough to let him slide through side-ways with the bag, his patience matching the intricacy and soft-ness of the embroidery on the shawl he carried.

Parveen Dyers is in the heart of Lajpat Nagar. Once we had turned off the main road into the market, the streets narrowed and the shops crowded in, one on top of another, layers of tiny businesses fighting for air. Above a milk shop was a typewriter reconditioner who shared space with an electric fan seller. Next door a sweet shop had a bubbling vat of syrup pushed right up against a great spitting pan of oil. And while the neighbouring samosa maker plied his trade, the sweet-shop man dropped curls of dough into the bubbling syrup.

The large flat roof above Parveen Dyers was laced with drying lines hung with shawls. Two men walked between the flying shawls, twitching them straight as they twisted and wrinkled on the lines, and then pulling down dry ones and replacing them with others from a large soggy pile on the edge of the roof.

Yaseen parked the car opposite the shop at an acute angle to the street. Three children on the corner laughed and pointed.

'Come, there is much in the dicky.' He opened the boot and took out three large piles of undyed shawls and another small crumpled plastic bag. 'I am honey man, you will see.' He laughed as he piled me with pashminas. 'One thing, please to call Mr Surinder, the owner, Lālājī.'

I nodded. Lālājī is a sycophantic form of address for a shop-keeper and has become an insult when said in a throw-away tone of voice. It was not a word I would normally have used but I did not wish to defy Yaseen.

Mr Surinder was sitting in a glass-sided office. His desk was layered in dyeing charts, some of them pages of tiny squares of colour, others large bundles of fabric bound as books, the edges frayed into colouring-box fringes of thread. I watched the old man through the wall of windows while we waited our turn. We were just a few feet from him, only separated by the glass, but he did not acknowledge our presence. He was a great bullfrog of a man, his head encased in a red cotton cap, his shirt and shawl – also red – wrapped tightly round his bulk. A glass of tea steamed in front of him. Thin boys dressed only in *lungi*, or loincloths, ran in and out of his office, carrying small pots of dye from the boiling vats for the old man to test. He dipped a piece of white cloth into each and then shuffled among his charts to find the colour that it was supposed to match. Some of the test pots he waved away. To others he would add a different dye, taken from his colour library of tins behind him. With a large battered spoon he stirred in the one that he had picked, then tried another small piece of cloth in the test pot. His movements were fast and exact in spite of the size of his spilling, rumpled body. Then he paused for a moment, looked up and waved to one of his assistants to bring us in.

Yaseen scuttled around the old man's desk and presented the crumpled plastic bag that he had taken from the dicky.

'Lālājī, it is so good to see you. I am the honey man for you.' He

The pashmina drying lines of Lajpat Nagar

held out a jar of amber honey, its sides smudged because the lid did not fit properly and the honey had spilt.

Lālājī did not look very impressed. 'How kind.' He took the pot from Yaseen and passed it to one of his assistants, then wiped his hands on his shirt with a faint air of distaste.

I approached the desk.

'Lālājī, it is a pleasure to meet you. I have seen a lot of your work. I would like to talk to you but I know that you are a very busy man. Perhaps there will be a time when you are not quite so busy.'

'We are always busy,' he replied, still wiping his hands.

'I would be very grateful if you could find some time because I would like to talk to you about your business.'

'Maybe after New Year.' He smiled for the first time.

It was the second week of September.

'Are you from America?' he asked.

'No, I am from England.'

'From?'

'London.'

'London proper or London outer?'

'London proper, I suppose.'

'I was in England in 1980, in Birmingham. My brother has a most successful and good dentist practice there.' His smile was now wide and mostly toothless.

Another boy in a *lungi* came in with a test pot. The old man did not even take a piece of cloth. He just ran the liquid dye off the spoon and peered at the colour before waving the pot away. The sun came through and images of passing cyclists were fractured by one of the broken window panes. Behind us, on the other side of the glass partition, great copper dyeing vats simmered, stirred by boys with large sticks. Steam from the boiling dye shone on their naked torsos. Their foreheads were marked with coloured stripes so that they looked like so many sadhus. Sodden piles were pulled out of the great round pots and flopped on to the floor. One piece from each mound was then pulled free and pressed with an iron that sat heating on an ancient stove in the corner. Each small pressed section was carried to the old man in his office for another check. These sodden rags steaming on a chemically eroded cement floor were the same shawls that would be rinsed, finished, bought, shipped and then slipped around the necks of high-maintenance, gamin-fringed blondes to keep them warm as they clippety-clipped from the aura massage clinic to a blue-fin tuna sushi lunch with the girls. At Parveen Dyers the pile of shawls smelt of wet dog.

'I was born in what we are now calling Pakistan in the year 1931. You have been to Pakistan?' the old man asked.

'No, I have not. I know it is impossible, but would you like to see Pakistan again?'

He laughed and waggled his hand.

'I was coming here in 1947 with so many of Hindus.'

I looked over to Yaseen. His expression was inscrutable.

'It was such a journey,' Mr Surinder went on. 'I do not think I am wishing to make that one again. I was setting up dyeing business at Red Fort in 1950. We Hindus from Lahore are best of all dyers in India. You are knowing this thing?' He shouted for one of the boys. 'You will take tea?'

'Yes, please.' I signalled towards Yaseen.

Mr Surinder ignored the gesture and called for three *chai*. He had included Yaseen without any consultation.

'Now I am having three factories and this dyeing shop. We are fine business because whosoever is coming to us we will take in dyeing. Not like shops that are turning away small orders because not enough of money. We are looking after small man too. Our dyeing is of highest quality, manual dyeing. See, all this is manual labour.'

It was there all around us. Not a single piece of machinery was involved at any stage. Every piece was hand-dyed in the same way as when the Lahori dyeing-*wallahs* had first set up their famous dyeing shops after Partition, thin raw arms thrusting in and out of the boiling vats, the old man presiding over his chemical agents, spoon in hand, red hat on head.

'I have four children. My sons are here with me. See, I am naming shop after my eldest son. I am Surinder but I have called it Parveen Dyers for him.'

Parveen, son of Surinder, was a big man, taller than his father but just as wide. His handshake was firm and he offered his hand readily, unlike his father.

'My second son is having business in our factories. Sometimes he is here in shop, but most of the times he is at factories. You would be most interested to see my factories. I am thinking this would be a good plan.' He paused so that I could digest this information. 'There are two daughters. Elder one is top-flight anaesthetist. She is in United States. I was in her house with her there in 1993. All kinds of things in her house that are making my mind explode. She has machines for all things. Machine for taking juice out of fruits, machine for taking fruits out of juice and what all else. I was pressing wrong buttons all the time. Even dog was having a machine to let him in and out of house for going into the garden for doing his needful.' The old man pressed his fingers together in puzzlement. 'Dog was having big problem with machine, not making it work and all. Dog is getting upset, daughter is getting upset. So daughter takes dog to doctor for calming. This is a good thing. I am thinking it is bad for daughter if dog is upset. Dog is named Nandi. You know this? Nandi the vehicle of Shiva, great god Shiva, you know?'

Nandi was a bull.

'What kind of dog is Nandi?'

'Poodle dog,' the old man replied after some thought.

'Lālājī, do you think it will be possible to dye these shawls by the end of next week?' I asked, trying to steer the conversation back to business.

The old man affected deep concentration and pressed his index fingers to his temples.

'I am consulting my son on this.' He beckoned to Parveen who was involved with a mound of wet shawls out by the vats. Parveen nodded, an affirmative nod, a particular gesture, a little sharper than the standard head weave that tends to mean nothing in particular. Yaseen sighed. I smiled, trustingly accepting the promise of prompt delivery, and the old man adopted the dignified pose of a great benefactor.

'After this order we will be having no time. Parveen son is holidaying in Goa. We will be closing shop for some time. Parveen son is going to best five-star resort in Goa. You know Goa?'

'I hope to go there for a bit before the New Year.'

'What resort will you be staying in?' he asked.

'Oh, quite a small one, a long way from any of the busy beaches.' I lowered my voice. 'Not many people go there.'

The old man smiled, satisfied that I must be going somewhere quiet, discreet and élite. I had no intention of disillusioning him by revealing that I was heading for a cluster of huts that were more New Age than cocktail umbrella.

Parveen waved for me to accompany him to the shop at the front of the building where the rest of the customers come to deposit their saris to be chemically reinvented. Behind a long grey formica counter two boys stitched, attaching small cotton tags to every garment that came into the shop. Each tag was coded with the initials of the owner. Until things were tagged they were not even in the queue for the dyeing vats.

Yaseen leant over.

'Maybe small gift for the tagging-*wallahs* could help make the movement of your shawls more smooth.'

I thought to protest but did not. This was the currency of business in India.

'What do you think would be suitable?' I asked.

'Some sweets would be good idea.'

The two boys with the flying needles were very thin. Some sweets might do them good. We left the shop and tramped the well-worn path to the Bengali Sweet Market at the end of the road, Yaseen walking three paces ahead.

I decided to order a box of *barfi*, the standard milk fudge, the mainstay of India's *mithai*, or sweet, sellers. I chose a plain two-pound box and was about to ask the server to pick out the pieces when Yaseen coughed.

'Do you think this is right?' I asked him.

He peered at the box.

'There are many workers, perhaps four pounds.' He stepped towards the counter, waving away the smaller box that I had selected and pointing to the larger size. His hand hovered over various trays and then swiftly and decisively he signalled to the server which ones were required – some green, some pink, some pale chocolate brown with silver paper on top. Each tray that Yaseen pointed to was more expensive than the last. He ordered twice, three and then four times as much as I had originally intended. He was giving me a lesson in business strategy. Future dealings with the front-of-house boys at Parveen Dyers would be judged on the quality of the *barfi* that I was about to buy. Yaseen was racking up a bill equivalent to a month's salary for one of the taggers. He assured me it would stand me in good stead. He took particular care to make sure that the box was tied up with a large amount of gold ribbon and twiddly bows.

I paid and Yaseen handed the box to me. I carried it back to the dyers and handed it over to the tagging boys. They put it to one side without any acknowledgement and carried on with their work. Yaseen looked pleased. He whispered that we had achieved much and that now was the time to leave. Though there were colour charts that I would have liked to check they would have to wait.

Whilst saying almost nothing Yaseen had controlled the whole meeting, from choosing to ignore the slight disdain of the old man and his son to overseeing the twists and twirls of the gold ribbon in the *mithai* shop. My presence had been incidental. The shawls would be tagged, he had been assured. They would go to the dyeing vats the following day. Yaseen had achieved his aim.

When we got back to the National Cottage Emporium Manzoor was in full flow.

'My son, here is my son.' Manzoor pulled the boy's ear, rubbed his cheek and then drew him to his side.

'Say hello to this lady. Best customer to your father. Say hello, Ahsan.'

The boy was a smaller, smoother-skinned replica of his father. He looked at me but did not speak. I smiled but there was no reaction.

'Ahsan, say hello,' his father entreated.

Ahsan maintained his silence.

'Hello, Ahsan,' I tried.

Still he did not speak.

'I thought your sons were at college in England,' I said to Manzoor.

'Ah yes, indeed you are right on this, but that is number one and number two son. This is number three son. He is too young at this time to be at special college.' Manzoor put his hand gently on his son's shoulder.

There was no sign of annoyance at the boy's refusal to speak. Manzoor adored his children. They were his irreproachable gifts from Allah. The conversation continued to centre around his son, his passion for cricket, his excellent performance at school in Srinagar – all such fine preparation for his entrance to the Mancunian college of orthodox Islam. Manzoor asked his son questions for my benefit, first in English and then in Kashmiri. At last the child replied, and Manzoor translated his school record, his latest cricket score, his enthusiasm for the Pakistan cricket captain. With each reply Manzoor leant over and stroked his son's head. There was no word about pashmina or the meeting with the dyer.

I needed to leave but wanted to know if we could get a delivery date from Parveen. Manzoor waved the subject away.

'When I am with my son there is no need for talking business,' he explained.

It was agreed that we would resume the following day.

'But tomorrow is Sunday. For some people this is a day of rest,' I appealed.

'Ah, but you are not understanding. I am a slave to my children.' Manzoor beamed and then tilted his head with a softer smile of sympathy for an unmarried woman.

Ahsan was still with his father on Sunday when I arrived at the shop and still we did not talk of business.

'Soon my sons will be returning from England. Then we are all taking ourselves to Kashmir for the time of Ramadan, most beautiful of times for my people.'

'When does Ramadan start?'

Manzoor thought for a moment.

'With new moon of December.'

'That's not for three months,' I said.

'This is true, but there is so much of things to prepare.'

'Who will be left in Delhi when you go back to Kashmir?'

'Brother number three, Ashraf, will be here and number four brother, Saboor, he is coming to Delhi from Srinagar. Yaseen also will be here to make all things perfect for you. Come to Kashmir. It is beautiful, best time, unbelievable.'

'I would like to but I am going back to London for a few weeks at the end of November. I must have all the things dyed by Parveen before I go. Do you think they will be ready in time? He promised to finish them by the end of next week.'

Manzoor sat and thought, his long fine fingers steepled together. He puffed and popped his mouth as he considered.

'Please to remember that we have festivals of Dussehra and Diwali coming up and this will be meaning every grand lady in whole of city will be dyeing every sari she is having in her cupboard. Parveen is very best dyer and he will be having so much of work. Be sure of this, we will get your shawls as soon as is possible even if I am having to go and speak with Parveen myself.' He paused for a moment to give me time to take in the significance of his offer. Manzoor, eldest of the Wangnoo brothers, would himself speak to the dyer in Lajpat Nagar.

'More than this,' he continued, 'if Parveen is not sending these pieces back by time I am thinking to go to Kashmir, I, Manzoor, will come with you to Parveen Dyers.'

By the beginning of November the shawls had still not come back from Parveen Dyers, and by now Manzoor had bought his ticket for Srinagar.

This time it was Manzoor who drove us to Lajpat Nagar. He had elected to drive because he had just bought a new car in preparation for the arrival of his youngest brother Saboor. Manzoor wanted to test-drive baby brother's new car.

A blue Maruti, the new people-mover of middle-class India, was parked outside the Wangnoos' godown in Sujan Singh Park. As Delhi godowns go, it is about as chic as you can get. Sujan Singh Park is a 1930s Art Deco building just across the road from Khan market, the top-of-the-range bazaar where all the expatriates and diplomats go to shop. Their servants go to the back of the market, to the grocers and vegetable-sellers where they can buy beef tomatoes imported from Spain and basil grown in palace gardens in Rajasthan. And while they do so the employers park their four-wheel drives at the front and go and buy Versace jeans and compact disks.

Occasionally there is a dispute over a parking space. I had once seen a Delhi matriarch square up to a diplomat's wife. Eventually the Delhiite lost her temper and attacked the supposedly diplomatically immune wife, yanking her from her car by her hair and giving her a good thrashing in front of a delighted crowd of shoppers. The story dominated the Delhi papers for days.

The Wangnoo brothers do not shop at Khan market. The prices offend their sensibilities, and the shop assistants can be off-hand with Kashmiris, sometimes even refusing to serve them. In their eyes one Kashmiri is much like another and they do not believe that any of them have sufficient means to shop there. They do not take the time to see whether there is a Mont Blanc pen nestling in an upper pocket, a Rolex on the wrist or Gucci loafers under the hem of the *feron*.

At Sujan Singh Park, Manzoor swung the keys of the new Maruti on his finger as we left the godown.

'Look at this. Tell me it is not beautiful. Come, see interior. It is finest in all India.' He unlocked the car with gravitas.

The tinted windows did lend the Maruti a certain mystery but this was dispelled as soon as the door was opened. Every single surface was sealed in plastic.

Manzoor ran his hand over the industrially sheathed dashboard. 'Unbelievable,' he murmured.

We stood and waited until he felt that we had been given enough time to drink in the wonders of the vehicle, then he pulled forward the driver's seat to let Yaseen and me into the back. As we swung out of the gates at speed I shot across the plastic-covered back seat and ended up hard against Yaseen's shoulder. He pushed me away gently but quickly as Manzoor pulled out into the Khan market traffic without so much as a glance in his wing mirror.

'See how this takes to the road, just like champion,' said Manzoor as he took the next heart-stopping corner. 'My Ahsan, my boy, do you not think he is good-looking?' He turned to face me as he spoke, his profile outlined by the fender of an oncoming truck.

My reply was drowned by the siren scream of the truck's horn.

As Manzoor swerved the new Maruti back on to the right side of the road, the truck lurched out of our path. 'You see, Allah is good, always watching us,' he announced with a backward glance.

Yaseen sat in silence.

'Now you have met my Ahsan, you will come to Kashmir to meet rest of family when all parts are joined for Ramadan.' He paused to change gear. 'If you are coming in December the snows will be all over, whole valley will be white. Unbelievable but so much of things you will not be seeing on account of snow. You will have to come back again in spring and summertime. This is truly beautiful time. You must come for time when willow is cut.'

'Willow?' I asked.

'Willow, of course willow. Did you never take the road south from Srinagar to Anantnag?'

I could not remember.

'Little, little shops all along this road. How can you have been missing them? They make finest *kerket* bats. They are cutting willow in spring when the snow is first melting, before the sap is coming up. Best time for cutting, when the snows from Siachen Glacier makes river flow blue of our Kashmir sky.' Manzoor ground the gears again. 'So much of trouble up on glacier, so much of death.'

Yaseen nodded in agreement.

'But is still early time in spring and willow has little of sap from before the snow, enough for keeping "tock" for hitting of balls.' Manzoor made the sound of leather off willow. 'But not yet new sap to make too soft.'

The Siachen Glacier lies high in the north-east of Kashmir, Pakistan to its north, the area ceded by Pakistan to the Chinese to the north-east, and the line of control with India to the south. Snow-melt turns the Kashmiri rivers blue, but it does not wash the blood from the heights of the glacier that have been tainted by conflict.

'When you are coming to Kashmir you will meet my good friend Mr Hakim. He is most famous and world-renowned maker of *kerket* bats. His father was making bats for Indian teams and Johnny Sahib teams in times before Partition. You would not believe how many bats were coming out of such small shop. Everyone is knowing my friend Mr Hakim. People coming from all over world to buy his bats. Mr Viv Richards was coming on special visit to buy bats.'

'How many did he buy?' I asked.

'He is still coming, Hakim tells me, he is still coming soon, very soon. But worse thing of all is Hakim is having to hide his bats away because of militants making life so bad for my friend. They are beating him and saying for him to give them free bats. Peoples coming from all over world to buy Hakim's bats but bad militants just taking them.' Manzoor took both his hands from the wheel and clasped his head. Fortunately we were stationary.

By the time we reached Parveen Dyers Manzoor was in a feverish state over the plight of Mr Hakim. The shawl hangers on the roof of the shop laughed at his casual parking, half way across the road. Manzoor ignored the jangle and shouts of passing cyclists who were having to reroute because of the jutting Maruti. He strode across the road and into Mr Surinder's fishbowl office. Yaseen and I hovered in his wake.

As Manzoor entered the office his whole demeanour changed, even his posture. He stooped in front of the old man, his tone softened and he looked at the ground in front of Mr Surinder's feet.

'Lālājī, my best greetings to you. I hope that you are finding our special honey from Kashmir is sweet for you.' Manzoor spoke in Hindi.

The old man was wearing a different-coloured hat, its petrol blue echoing his choice of dove-grey shirt and gunmetal shawl. He peered over his desk. There was a look of mild surprise on his face. He had not been expecting the senior Wangnoo brother.

'What can bring you to my humble shop?' he asked.

'I come in great hope that you will be able to dye all shawls for this good lady, VVIP customer of National Cottage Emporium. She has to get back to London in time for end of November. She is taking shawls for Queen and her family in England.'

Mr Surinder, Yaseen and I were wide-eyed. Manzoor was unashamed.

The shawls were delivered on time.

CHAPTER 4

Hot Pink
of Notting Hill

ONCE THE SHAWLS for the Queen of England had been dyed, Manzoor flew to Srinagar. I was left in the soft November light of the city to pack up bundles to send and carry to London.

Just before I left Delhi, Gautam asked me who I thought was going to buy pashmina.

'People like me,' I replied.

'What do you mean people like you? You look like a hippie.'

'That's just what I mean. What looks like hippie to you is what people are wearing in London now.'

'And you really think they will want to buy shawls?'

He did not seem to have much confidence in my selling skills.

'We will raise money for DRAG and the schools, I promise.'

Gautam gave me piles of information about DRAG, lovingly written leaflets charting the progress of the women and children in education groups he had set up with his fellow-workers, stories of hope, tiny victories, the desperate sense of futility in pitching a small organization against such an ocean of need.

Leaflets and fact sheets were packed carefully among the layers of pashmina that I was sending back to London in advance. It was the closest the slum children of DRAG would come to pashmina. It was also the closest the people who were going to buy the shawls would come to the cause that they were supporting at one remove. Then the documents and the shawls were stitched up together in hessian bags for dispatch to England – duty paid, passport number given, addresses, Delhi and London, mother's maiden name, father's profession, sign once, twice, thrice and Heathrow-bound.

Gautam and I met once more before I left. It was at a lecture at the Indian International Centre, the meeting-ground of the political establishment, the business élite and those members of India's erstwhile royal families who have managed to redirect themselves away from gin and thing and into commerce and government.

In the anonymous semi-darkness of the auditorium I sat next to an elderly gentleman. He seemed uncomfortable about being so close to me, planting his walking-stick between us and staring at it, marking out his territory. Then he took a large white handkerchief from his pocket and spread it over his knees, smoothing all the creases away with long slow strokes. He folded it and then began the smoothing process again. After looking at it for a while, he turned to look at me, pursed his lips and unfolded it. This time he spread it out on the arm-rest between his seat and mine. He spent even longer flattening it out to its full size. Once finished, he leant back from his work and surveyed the barrier that he had laid out between us. He was not satisfied. He picked up his handkerchief for the third time, plucking it from the centre until he had created a small tented effect on the arm-rest. Finally he settled back into his seat, still keeping an eye on his handkerchief and occasionally glancing in my direction to check that I was observing the boundaries.

I got up, careful not to disturb his labours, and crossed the aisle to another empty seat. He looked sadly at the seat I had left, his hand fluttering over his small white cotton tent. Then he snapped it up and folded it away into his pocket, his face expressionless.

Gautam found me in the gloom and sat down beside me. He pointed to characters in the audience, an ex-minister, the ex-minister's ex-wife next to him, in what was apparently a very comfortable arrangement; a writer recently returned from having collected virtually every major literary award across the globe; a Bollywood actress who had slid into politics. The latter had once played the concubine of a prince who, having reduced him to virtual slavery with her physical ingenuity, set herself up at the head of his court. Her physical ingenuity was not, of course, shown in the film, only hinted at. However, the actress was believed to have borrowed from the role in pursuit of her newfound career.

I pointed to the man with the handkerchief.

'Who is that over there?'

Gautam looked surprised.

'Do you know him?' he asked.

'After a fashion.'

'He was the deputy prime minister.' He gave me the dates and the political era. My erstwhile neighbour had once held the reins of power at a time when his superior had been profoundly unpopular with the electorate. Now the former deputy prime minister sat in the semi-darkness with a walking-stick and a handkerchief.

On the stage Ramu Gandhi, the Mahatma's grandson, stood up to introduce the speakers. He wore a scarf of yellow *khadi* around his neck, the simple homespun weave championed by his grandfather as the fabric of Indian society.

'Let us wish our neighbour Pakistan a happy . . .', he paused, '. . . future.'

That year, 1998, was the fiftieth anniversary of the UN ceasefire in Kashmir. No one was optimistic about the immediate future of dialogue between the two nations. In May that year, in the desert of Rajasthan at Pokhran, India had detonated three nuclear devices buried in the earth. Rocks weighing a thousand tons had been vaporized. A scientist watching the test had said, 'I can now believe the stories of Lord Krishna lifting a hill.'

Pakistan had responded with a similar test. The global police had leapt into the fray. And now, six months later, Gandhi's grandson was on stage at the Indian International Centre to pass judgement.

He puffed his cheeks into the folds of his *khadi*.

'This stockpiling of nuclear weapons is a global show of juvenile delinquency. We in India have had a tantrum.'

There was total silence in the auditorium. He waited until the stillness was about to erupt, reached for a glass of water and drank most of it as we all watched.

'Telling the truth is profoundly dehydrating.' He finished the glass. 'Our tests in the desert are tantrums, but then tantrums are not always such a bad thing. We allow our teenage children to have them because they are a part of their development. We know that it is a part of their learning.

'So the great global police have been having their tantrums for fifty years and no one judged them and now, like AIDS, we have caught the nuclear disease.' He paused again. Still no one moved. 'Every power that holds nuclear weapons has the blood of Hiroshima on its hands. And now the West is telling us that we are in danger of using Kashmir as a nuclear trigger. Does the West have any real understanding of our valley? Does it have the right to play King Solomon?'

There was a cry from the audience. Others joined in until there was a chorus of snorted, grunted and coughed agreement from the floor. Looking across at the former deputy prime minister I saw him begin to heave himself out of his chair, leaning all the while on his walking-stick. He was a tall though now stooped man, and his slow progress through the auditorium was noted, each of his laboured steps marked by the heavy fall of his walking-stick as it beat out a slow roll of disapproval. Then the audience turned back to listen to the first of the speakers.

As we crossed to the bar after the end of the discussion, Ramu Gandhi was just ahead of us. Gautam knew him from his days as a newspaper editor. He introduced us. Mr Gandhi had a strong, long handshake. He continued to hold on to my hand as we passed along the corridor of necessary pleasantries.

'Miss Hardy is hoping to go up to Kashmir when she comes back to India next month,' Gautam volunteered.

'Ah well, we all know that you Brits have a tendency to be foolish,' Mr Gandhi replied. 'Why would you want to go to Kashmir at this time?'

'I am buying pashminas from some of the village weavers up there,' I explained.

'I am sure you will find it very profitable,' said Mr Gandhi with a blank look. 'I believe pashmina is a very luxuriant thing, but I must admit to having a preference for *khadi*.' He was still holding my hand and, for the first time, I began to feel uncomfortable, looking down at his locked fingers instead of at his rumpled face. He dropped my hand immediately.

'Ah, the lady does not find this comfortable. I think you will be finding Kashmir even less so,' Mr Gandhi said.

I blushed, and Gautam looked embarrassed by my gauche behaviour.

'We are all so greedy, do you not think? Perhaps there is no need for you to buy pashmina from Kashmir. Perhaps there will be a more needful, more balanced time when you could return there.' Mr Gandhi walked slightly ahead of us.

'She is helping to support my NGO, the schools in the Delhi slum areas,' Gautam jumped in.

'Ah, very worthy,' rumbled Mr Gandhi.

'She is writing and making documentaries as well,' Gautam continued, nobly championing my cause.

Mr Gandhi turned towards me as we walked into the bar.

'Miss Hardy, you are packing a great many things into your life. You must have mastered the art of thinking consciously as you sleep, a very great skill.' He shook my hand but this time he did not hold on to it. Then he rewound the *khadi* about his neck and nodded to Gautam. 'But perhaps you are also playing with fire.'

It was a closing comment. He walked away to his corner of the packed bar, to an empty chair that was always left for him, where he sat and drank alone. Mr Gandhi was the philosopher-in-residence.

The heaviest snowfall for fifty years fell in Kashmir the night before I left Delhi in mid-November, or so they said. Most of the villages to the north of Srinagar were cut off and the electricity supply failed across the valley. A state of emergency was declared. An Indian army spokesman, a tall Sikh major in a camouflage-green turban, made the official announcement that conditions were so bad it would not be possible to make supply drops to the villages. The army would have its hands full simply maintaining its position at various points along the Line of Control between India and Pakistan. Some commentators shook their heads and said that the Sikh major had given away too much information, just the kind of thing Pakistan wanted to hear. The usual political arguments broke out while the mountain villages went without food and light.

In London, the autumn had been muggy and the city was in the grip of a strain of 'flu that had propagated merrily in the damp warmth. The weather turned just after I arrived, freezing the colour from late roses and turning them to sepia.

Usually there was just a big pile of bills when I got back and perhaps a couple of invitations to weddings or parties that had been and gone. This time it was different. I had sent a few post-cards during the weeks before I left Delhi to carefully selected friends with finely tuned shopping habits. I had told them that I was coming back laden with pashmina. The result was that the usual pile of bills was dwarfed by cards, notes and faxes asking for sneak previews. The ansaphone had been switched back on a couple of days before my return by a friend and now held fifty-three messages. Three people had left no message. Five calls were from family. The rest were requests for pashmina and when I had listened to them all I looked in despair at my luggage scattered around me on the floor. The shawls that I had sent on ahead had not yet arrived. I had no value without the goods. I pressed the delete button without writing down any of the messages.

Three days later four hessian bales were delivered to me at ten o'clock at night out of the boot of a fifteen-year-old Ford Escort van with one crumpled wing. The Wangnoos had managed to find a courier company that was acceptable to them. It was cheaper than the big international companies and it was owned by a cousin of a wife of a cousin.

The driver of the van was also apparently a cousin. He was studying at the London School of Economics and he helped with deliveries out of hours to repay his uncle for providing bed and board in Asian London suburbia. We negotiated on the price for a while and he gave me a small discount for paying cash.

My luggage was still scattered around the flat in various states of unpack. I cut into the hessian bales and let the shawls fly. By midnight every chair, table, sofa and suitcase was draped. The Delhi bazaar had come to West London.

There was also a familiar, less welcome smell. The shawls had come with a hint of Parveen Dyers about them. I stayed up until four o'clock in the morning trying to iron the chemical smell out of them and then slept surrounded by images of Lajpat Nagar.

'Hello.'

It was Robin, ringing to rouse me from dreams of Delhi.

'Welcome back. Good flight?'

'Terrible.'

'Poor you. Have you got the shawls?'

'Yes.'

'Good. Now I've met a rather nice-looking woman who has one of those smart shops in Hungerford. Just the sort of person we want flogging pashmina, don't you think?'

'I'm sorry, I've still got jet-lag, I have been away for eight months, I have not even talked to any of my family yet. Can I have a bit of time to sort myself out, please?'

'Fine. Let's talk later.'

'No, I'll call soon and we can arrange a proper meeting.'

'All right. Bye.' He crashed down the telephone as he always does.

The following morning there was a piece in one of the gossip columns about Mr and Mrs Tom Cruise and how Hollywood's Midas couple loved London. Mrs Cruise, or rather Ms Kidman, admitted to a passion for pashmina. 'I've got fifty of them and there are still more colours I'd like,' she was reported as saying.

As I left the flat I could hear the telephone ringing. I ignored it. Then, walking down Holland Park Avenue, there came a familiar shout.

'Hey, Justine, come here.' It was a New Yorker who I bumped into from time to time in shops in the neighbourhood.

'Come on, get over here.' She was in a large car and she had stopped in the middle of the road. A traffic jam began to build up behind her. 'You've got pashmina. I just know you've got pashmina.'

Horns began to blow but she ignored them.

'I have to have one now. Hot pink, I have to have a hot pink one. You have my number. Call me, you have to call me.' She stuck her tongue out at the driver behind who had been sitting on his horn and then screeched away.

I stood red-faced on the pavement and shrugged my shoulders at the irate driver. Still, I did call her as soon as I got home. She was too frightening, too New York, for me not to.

'Great, so you have hot pink?'

'Yes, I have.'

'I'll take three. What other colours have you got?'

'Most colours.'

'Fabulous! Okay, do this. Come round here with a whole bunch of them. I'm gonna call a gang of girlfriends. I know they all want pashmina. It will be fun. So tomorrow or Thursday, which can you do?'

'Thursday afternoon.'

'Right, that's good for me too. Three o'clock and bring loads of them, we all want lots.'

Her house was big. If it had been in the middle of the countryside it would still have looked substantial but in the middle of Holland Park, with its double gates, double garage and double front door with two large brass knobs, it seemed vast. There were box trees on either side of the doors set in glass cubes, the trees shorn to rigid topiary to match the cubes. A pair of stone greyhounds sat in heraldic pose in front of the trees.

Each time I lugged one of the baskets of pashmina from my car up the steps to the front door, a security camera swivelled and blinked at me. When I rang the bell another camera opened and its shutter flashed.

A well-dressed woman answered the door. I introduced myself. She looked down on me from the top step. Her trousers were well cut and she wore a good pink cashmere cardigan. I was wearing clothes suitable for lugging around baskets of pashmina. My outfit did not impress the woman in pink cashmere. She watched as I carried the baskets, one by one, through to where I was supposed to be setting out my wares.

The sitting-room was the size of my whole flat. Everything was large, swollen sofas banked up with too many cushions and investment paintings on a grand scale on the walls. Most of the furniture

My sales wares

looked as if it had come straight from the cabinet-maker who had recently become the darling of London's interior designers. The exception was a low oriental table in front of the fireplace. On it lay four piles of books, one to a corner, each a squared-off stack of hardback catalogues from art exhibitions around the world.

While I gawped, the housekeeper came back with a black lacquered tray. There were matching bowls of Japanese rice crackers and out-of-season cherries, plates of sushi and some tiny blueberry muffins. She arranged them carefully and symmetrically between the four piles of art books.

'Please, do help yourself,' she said in a tone implying the contrary.

Hot-pink New York came in as I was about half way through unpacking the baskets. In contrast to her house, her box trees and her housekeeper, New York was looking casual. In fact she was one of the scruffiest dressers in the neighbourhood. It was one of her redeeming features.

She was talking on a portable telephone. She mouthed 'Hi' and ducked down to collect some sushi and a couple of the dolly-sized blueberry muffins from their black lacquered bowls. With the telephone squashed between her ear and a hunched shoulder, and the sushi and muffins in one hand, she began to whip shawls out of bags at speed. The sushi and the muffins went into her mouth and now, with both hands free, she began to wind shawls around herself. Once draped she went over to a mirror above the large fireplace to inspect herself.

'This colour is terrible. It does nothing for me. Look, it just dies on me, it makes me look so washed-out.'

She was washed out. The pretty summer sky shawl was cast aside.

'Now this I quite like. No, I change my mind, it's not there, it's just two steps off the colour I need.'

Crushed raspberry joined sky blue on the floor.

'You know, when I say hot pink I mean really full on. That is just kinda ugh.' She poked her toe at the now very crushed raspberry.

I gathered up the rejects and started to refold them.

'Oh, don't bother with all that stuff. Everyone will do exactly the same as me.' She took the shawls from me and threw them on to the nearest sofa.

'God, they look fantastic! I'm gonna have to buy a few that I can just throw around the place. You know, just muzz them up on the furniture.' She muzzed sky blue and crushed raspberry around the cushions.

'See, now how great does that look?'

Two crumpled shawls on an over-stuffed sofa.

Half an hour later there were about thirty crumpled shawls muzzed together on the same sofa. I was crouched in one corner over an invoice book, trying to pick squashed blueberry muffin out of the fringe of a bleached lemon shawl while writing out an invoice for Belle from Austin, Texas. She had bought three shawls.

'The cream one is for me so you do not have to pack it up all fancy and such. It works with ma face. The pink is for ma brother Henry and the lilac is for his significant other, Charles. He just looks a dream in all those mauvey things. I'm just gonna get mad if I only have one. I'm gonna have to buy a whole load more.'

She pronounced lilac as if it were two words and most of the others she managed to stretch to about four. It was a long time since I had been around a Texan drawl deep enough to swim in.

'Ma family has a ranch, you know. It is one of the most renowned in the state. Night times when we are out it can seem awful cool. You know these pashminas are gonna save ma life.'

Another tough New Yorker, currently soaring in business circles, was holding court on the other side of the room. Her baby daughter was keen for her attention but was being held in check by an au pair who, the New Yorker explained, was from Bosnia. Bolting handfuls of Japanese crackers, her large diamond ring clinking against the lacquer bowl each time, Ms Corporate New York launched into her experiences of recent house-hunting in Manhattan and Notting Hill.

'You all just have no idea the stuff that I have been through. It's disgusting the way you get treated by these realty kids. God, I mean I'm old enough to be their mother. What do I get to show me around a place with a two-million tag? Some spotty geek with a rah-rah accent who tells me exactly how bad his hangover is. Then he deigns to take off his shades and he thinks he can smell money and he goes all humble and apologetic. So I say, "Listen honey, get in the car, get over your hangover and remember I know that you work on commission. It doesn't take a Nobel Prize winner to work out the percentage on two mill." He was a perfect pussycat after that.'

Ms Corporate New York and Austin Belle eyed each other across the lacquered tray of blueberry muffins. Belle smiled the frosty smile of an iced daiquiri. Ms Corporate responded with a display of deal-crunching, investment-capped teeth.

A tall, beautiful woman arrived. She was late and apologetic, and greeted everyone in the room including the Bosnian au pair. Most of the women did not warm to her. She was too thin, too pretty and too polite. As she admired the shawls she asked about India, Delhi and the slum children.

I asked whether she had any children.

'I have a boy and a four-month-old baby daughter.'

She was from Poland and had married an American whom she had met while modelling in New York.

'I just don't buy it that you've got a baby. You're too skinny. What did you do, get liposuction?' Ms Corporate New York smiled as she spoke, but it was not a warm smile. 'Come on, we need proof. Where's the kid?'

'My husband has her, and my son,' replied the Polish woman.

'Oh great, perfect body, perfect life and a husband who likes to child-mind. I guess you never had zits and you've got a law degree.'

Ms Corporate New York was joking now but the Polish woman did not smile.

'We are getting divorced and he has taken the children because he has a very clever lawyer.' She gave the facts in a flat voice.

The Bosnian au pair started to cry. Most of us had assumed that she did not speak much English because of the way her employer spoke in front of her. But she had been listening, understanding and absorbing it all. The Polish woman went to her and touched her face.

'I am sorry, I did not mean to upset you.'

'No, no, you are very beautiful woman and it is so sad for you.' The Bosnian girl hugged her small charge to her.

'She's so freaky sometimes. She doesn't say a thing for weeks and then she suddenly goes and cries all over everyone. Her brother was killed in Sarajevo by the bad guys,' whispered Ms Corporate New York, loud enough for me to hear on the other side of the room.

Everyone fell silent. A mobile phone rang and was answered immediately, a note of relief in the reply. The mood in the room relaxed.

'God, I have to have more pashmina parties. They are just so much fun.' My hostess popped one more blueberry muffin into her mouth and draped another shawl on top of the one she was already wearing.

A pretty woman who had made much less noise than the others rolled her eyes at me. She had been waiting quietly as I wrapped, packed and wrote for the less patient members of the gathering. As the others began to leave at various decibel levels she remained on one of the over-stuffed sofas, picking up crumbs from a blueberry muffin that her little boy had thrown over the fat cushions.

Our hostess left the room with the final flight of pashmina pur-chasers. The pretty woman and I were left alone in a nest of muzzed shawls and tissue paper.

'Not quite how we behave at shower parties back home,' she said. Her soft accent rolled like Bondi Beach spume.

'Hasn't pashmina fever hit Sydney yet?' I asked.

'It's just starting, but the prices are only for the truly rich and vacuous at the moment.'

She wore virtually no make-up, her skin was clear and her eyes were as blue as the shawl that she had picked out.

'Can I have this one please?'

'Of course you can.'

I had sold sixteen shawls. Ms Corporate New York with the two-million-pound house hadn't bought any, though she had tried them all on.

'Well, I bought a whole load from Nicole's guy a few months ago.'

Of course, she was a friend of Nicole.

By the end of November, just two weeks after my return from Delhi, Robin and I had sold a lot of our stock. It took me three hours to get through to Manzoor in Srinagar.

'*Salaam alekum*, how good to hear you. Business is very fine for you? We have been praying for this. It is our good wish.'

'Thank you, yes, business is good. I would like to make another order if possible and the sooner you can send it the better.'

'*Inshallah*, this will be possible. In two days my sons are coming from England college for time of Ramadan. I will be staying in Kashmir all this time. Yaseen is in Delhi. He will look after all your good needs while I am at my home. All things will be perfect, please be assured.'

'I'll send Yaseen an order with the bank's transfer confirmation at the end.'

'This is such very nice news. I am so happy to hear of this. All of news is fine, my children, the time of Ramadan and this order.

Allah is very great.' Manzoor sounded as if he was smiling as he spoke.

'I would like to get the shawls dyed in Kashmir if it is possible. I think your dyers in Srinagar produce a much better colour match than Parveen. How long would it take to get the shawls dyed in Kashmir?' I asked. The first shawls I had bought from Abdullah the storyteller had been dyed in Kashmir, their colours subtle and beautiful.

'Kashmir dyers are best in all of India. You are right on this. Maybe best in whole world. But problems we are having with much of snow. It is difficult to dye with so much of snow. And it is difficult for getting shawls from Kashmir to Delhi. Things are not so good at this time.' Manzoor glossed over the details when I questioned him as to why things were not so good.

A few days after our conversation I noticed a small paragraph in the foreign news section of my daily paper. It sat between a story about President Clinton and Buddy, his dog, and a brief report on an Italian pornography actress who had choked on a fishbone in a restaurant in Capri. Insurgents from Pakistan were believed to have occupied some of the Indian army outposts above Kargil, north-east of Srinagar. Personnel from the Indian army had apparently left their posts because of the severity of the weather and had taken shelter in the relative comfort of Kargil. The insurgents had been less sensitive about the weather. All flights in and out of the valley and all road traffic apart from military vehicles had been suspended. This was why it was not such a good time to be dyeing in Srinagar and trying to get shawls back to Delhi. The story was based on an unconfirmed report. It was not official news so it was not an official situation.

'What would you like for Kashmir?' I had asked Yaseen during one of our rally drives to Parveen Dyers in September.

'Azadi,' he had replied. *Azadi*, Kashmir's independence from Pakistan and India, a dream that was beginning to slide towards the realms of folklore.

'And what would *Azadi* mean to you?'

'This would mean that my sons would be true sons of our valley and that it would be our holy place with no more of politicians going chip chip all the time to make big money for their bad dealings. My valley for my people, Kashmir for Kashmiris.' He had touched his forehead to the steering wheel as he finished. I had not been able to see his face, to see whether his expression was one of sincerity or despair.

'Kashmir! Why are you buying all your stuff from there?' the loud New York pashmina party hostess had asked. 'They're just a bunch of terrorists up there. They grab tourists and murder them, for Christ's sake. Why do you want to support them? Have you gone Muslim or what?'

'No, I'm not a Muslim. I just buy the shawls from the Kashmiri weavers, many of whom have been pushed close to starvation by the loss of trade caused by the conflict.'

'But how do you know that the money doesn't get side-tracked into ammunition and stuff to blow up tourists? I don't want to subsidize people who are just a bunch of murderers.'

'They barely get enough money to buy food and other basic necessities, never mind arms. And you do not subsidize them. I buy the shawls from them. Your money goes towards educating the children in the Delhi slums.' I hoped I had not sounded as angry as I felt.

'And are the slum kids Muslim?' she had pushed on.

'I don't ask what religion they are.'

'Can't you tell?'

'Sometimes you can but it really isn't the kind of question you ask a five-year-old child when you're trying to encourage her to draw the things she dreams about.'

Ms Corporate New York had pricked up her ears at this point.

'So what do they draw? Do they do scary pictures of all the ugly stuff that happens to them?'

'They usually draw the same thing – a house, sometimes with a mountain in the background. There's usually water, a lake or a river, somewhere near the house and maybe some flowers, a tree, a cow or some goats.'

'That's not so imaginative.'

'They live in slums. They don't see those sorts of things much but their parents and relatives tell them about them.'

'Come on, they see houses, don't they? It's a city, isn't it?'

'Yes, they see houses and they see cows too, they see cows everywhere.'

'They have cows in the slums?' She had been amazed.

'If this was Delhi there would be cows in Holland Park too.'

'You mean you have cows in the street where you live?'

'Yes.'

'What is it with Delhi? Is it a city or a farmyard?'

Even as I told her about Hindus, and cows wandering the streets of Delhi with impunity, she had decided that I was subsidizing gun-running in Kashmir.

By the beginning of December Robin and I were in difficulties. When I lugged pashmina baskets back after a long day of selling I found curls of fax paper running off my desk. They were great missives from Robin, written in his usual trembling hand. What was I doing? How many had I sold? Was I ordering more? If not, why not? When would they arrive? What colours did I think would sell best? Were we getting the price right? Why were the shawls always late? There followed long reports on his sales progress. He had started to try to sell the shawls to the ladies who run bijou shops in the market towns of middle England. His problem came in trying to convince them. While it was easy for me to sell pashmina to a captive market literally on my doorstep, the Ma Griffe and baroque pearl-necklaced ladies of the home counties were harder to persuade. They had seen the shawls on the shoulders of a few high-maintenance wives of investment bankers, the new weekend additions to their coveted villages. But they were still not sure that the shawls did not look just like glorified rugs. Robin was trying to convert the politely interested manageresses among their shelves of lavender-scented drawer sachets and farm-made lemon curd. He warned them that to miss out on pashmina was to ignore a major new addition to the core wardrobe of every woman with style.

Robin wanted some tips on selling techniques. I was a woman, so he reasoned that I might have some inside tricks in selling to my own sex. We agreed to meet at his club on a Tuesday afternoon.

It was pouring with rain. I did not blow my horn at the chauffeur sitting resolutely on an expired parking-meter that was perfectly placed for me. I drove up beside him instead and waited. My intention must have been obvious and just to make sure he got the point I waved politely at him. He continued to ignore me, his nose deep in a book, as the rain battered his windscreen. I got out of the car and went round to tap on his window. He looked up with a familiar expression, the one worn by so many Delhi drivers when traffic-light beggars tap against their car windows.

I smiled.

His electric window slid down to precisely eye level and then stopped.

'Hello, I am sorry to interrupt your reading but I wondered if it would be possible to park on this meter.' I pointed to the single yellow line in front of us where he could safely park while he stayed in his car.

He shook his head and the window slid shut. I was getting wet. I tapped again. He looked out at me, still shaking his head. I did not shout but spoke loudly enough for him to hear me through the glass.

'I just hoped to be able to park on this meter as you have no credit on it. You could just as easily park on the yellow line so that I could use the meter.' By now my hair was sticking to my head and my clothes to my body.

The chauffeur smiled. Slowly and carefully he stuck two fingers up at me through his sealed window. I thanked him and parked a long way from the club, running back through the rain with pashminas for Robin clutched beneath my arm.

I arrived sodden, smelling of wet dog and not in the best of moods. The meeting with the chauffeur had made me late and Robin was already well settled.

'Hello, you're looking remarkably like one of your slum-dwellers. Is this a good look for a pashmina saleswoman?' He had a glass of water in one hand and a mixture of bread and olives in the other. When he kissed me I got a combination of all three on my cheek.

'Now,' he said, almost before I had sat down, 'I think I need to rethink my shawl-selling strategy. I'm not convinced that I'm showing them to their full effect.'

'Do you wear one when you go to see people about them?' I asked.

'Of course I do. You told me to. I do everything that you tell me to. Look, I've got it here.' He pulled one out from among the plastic bags he had nestling around his feet. A washed-out coral-coloured shawl emerged from among his purchases from Selfridges food halls, a little bit damp from the rain and tainted with the smell of jellied eels and rillettes. Robin knotted it around his neck.

I took it off, stood up, shook it out to its full size and folded it over once and then again across its width, using my raised knee to make the fold. Then I doubled it end to end and threw it around his neck, passing the two loose ends through the loop I had made. After a final tweak, I stood back to look at the effect.

'There, that is what is known in the trade as the Italian snuggle.'

Robin complete with the Italian snuggle

'I'm not sure that it's very convincing on me.' Robin tried to see himself in the mirror across the room.

'The Italian snuggle or you being able to sell shawls?'

'A bit of both really, I think.' Robin slumped back into the sofa.

'Perhaps you're going too much for the pile 'em high, sell 'em cheap routine.'

'Not easy to do when I've hardly got anything to sell.'

The meeting deteriorated. We had disagreed on selling techniques. Next we disagreed on our pricing policy.

'If we start trying to compete on price with big retailers we throw out our main advantage. If we bring down the price we devalue the fact that I am bringing back the very highest quality,' I said.

'I know that and you know that, but how does the average man on the street know?' Robin retorted.

I pulled the scarf from around his neck. It was now crumpled and smeared with bread and olives. But it was still exquisite and as soft as the storyteller's birds of paradise.

'Isn't it as simple as this?' I said. 'We have a beautiful product to sell and people want it. Either we accept that we operate in very different ways and try and be a bit more gentle with each other and get a nice little business going or we drive each other to the edge of the cliff and continue to argue as we jump.'

'Oh dear.' Robin looked surprised, his face falling.

'Why do you say that?'

'I just thought that it was all going so well, and then you turn around and say that it's all awful. How disappointing.'

'Oh come on, Robin, all we do is argue about every single point, whether it's colour, shape, size, price or sales technique. Have we agreed on one thing apart from the fact that we have a very good product?'

He looked at me with a hurt expression. 'Well, we argue a bit about it but we always have. It's healthy, good for business.'

'But so much of the bickering seems unnecessary,' I said.

'Rubbish, business is entirely about bickering. Keeps us on our toes.' And with that he popped some more bread and olives into his mouth.

CHAPTER 5

The Shadows
of the Valley

'DO PEOPLE FIGHT over them?' asked a Frenchwoman on the telephone.

'I'm not sure I know what you mean by "fight",' I replied. It was not long after the New York pashmina bee and I was still feeling bruised.

'I am calling from Paris. Pashmina shawls have just come to three shops here. When the first of them opened on Monday with the new stock there were hundreds of women queuing up outside. They just pushed and pushed. One woman fainted and had to be taken to hospital. It was horrible. Is it like that in London?' There was a note of distress in her voice.

'I assure you nothing like that happens here.'

'Oh, I am so pleased about this. Do you have private clients?'

'Well, yes, I suppose I do.' I had never thought of them as such.

'I think I will come to you from Paris,' she said.

'Were you planning to come to London anyhow?'

'No, but I would like to come now if you will take me as a private client.' Her plan was to be with me by seven in the evening, buy her shawls and catch the nine-thirty flight back.

Nadine was the perfect Parisienne, right down to her immaculately manicured fingernails. She threw her hands up in the air as she came through the door. Her flight had been delayed by two hours.

'You will not believe what they have done to me. Two hours round and around, one behind the other to land. I have seen every street around Heathrow a hundred times.'

Then she introduced herself and carefully took in the details of my flat.

'*C'est charmant.*' She managed to make it sound a bit like an insult. But then, after two hours of circling over outer London, she had every right to be slightly bad-tempered. It was ten o'clock at night and both of us would have liked to have been somewhere else.

I opened the pashmina trunk and she went to work. She was very thorough, sorting the colours that interested her on to one side and rejecting those she was not interested in and piling them back into the trunk. Some she hovered over and they became a separate pile for further examination. Her actions were systematic and fast.

'This one here, this is the colour of Bombay Sapphire.' She picked up a shawl. 'You know Bombay Sapphire? It is your stuff, you must know it.'

I had no idea what she was talking about.

'I'm sorry, I'm afraid I don't.'

'Do you drink?' she asked.

'What do you mean?'

'Bombay Sapphire, it is English gin with a picture of your funny old queen on it.'

'She's not that old,' I said defensively. 'After all, her mother is still alive.'

'No, no, not this one, much older, the short, fat one.'

'Oh, you mean Queen Victoria?'

'Yes, this is her. She looks like a frog.' Nadine paused. 'No, not a frog, I think a toad.' She giggled in an unParisienne fashion, openly and freely.

'I'm sorry but I still don't understand what you mean by Bombay Sapphire.'

95

'It is – oh I am not sure how to describe it – blue, like this, this blue. The bottle, I mean, not the gin.' She waved the shawl she was holding at me. It was the turquoise of English summer skies during those rare days of flaming June. At last I understood what she meant.

Nadine had been given my name by a friend in London. She knew that the money from the shawls went to the slum schools in Delhi.

'My brother is an ophthalmic surgeon. He was with Médecins sans Frontières for two years. He worked with a programme in South India. It was a travelling clinic that toured around villages removing cataracts. They have a terrible problem with this. You must know about it.'

I did. The high percentage of villagers with cataracts was the result of a vitamin deficiency, particularly during times of famine in deprived states such as Bihar and Andhra Pradesh.

'Is that where you heard about Bombay Sapphire?'

'No, no, my boyfriend likes it very much and I think the colour of the bottle is beautiful.'

Nadine bought four shawls, two of them the colour of Bombay Sapphire, but by then it was too late to catch the return flight that she wanted. Instead we walked up the road to a place that spit-roasts chicken until the skin is puffed to perfect crispness. She ate with her fingers and smoked unfiltered Gauloise cigarettes, picking the stray tobacco off her tongue in the way film stars used to in the Forties. She told me about her alcoholic boyfriend and her mother who trained racehorses for the flat and groomed men for politics. I liked her and was happy to drive her to the airport with her four shawls.

Robin had had a new idea. He rang me at seven o'clock the next morning.

'Hi!'

'Good morning, Robin. You obviously had a quiet Saturday night.'

'Nope, I was out dancing until two this morning. Usual thing, very good party, sold another two, can't remember who to. I've been up for ages. What about you?' He was irritatingly awake.

'I sold four last night.'

'Rubbish!'

'A lovely girl came over from Paris just to buy shawls. She said they were all sticking their fingers in each other's eyes in the rue de Montaigne to get hold of them.'

'You clever girl.'

'We had a lovely time. She ate chicken with her fingers and managed to smoke at the same time.'

'What?'

'Don't worry, it's too early in the morning. Did you just ring to ask me whether I had sold any since we last spoke?'

'No, I've been thinking about names.'

'Do we need to rush? And do we have to discuss it at this time in the morning?'

'Unless we give it a name and file it at Companies House within the next couple of months we'll be trading illegally. So what about the Pashmina Company or the Pashmina Trading Company?'

'Goat,' I replied.

'What do you mean "Goat"?'

'They come from goats.'

'It's not very catchy, and it's a bit short, don't you think?'

I heard the rustle of sheets as Robin rearranged himself.

'I thought you said you'd been up for hours.'

'I have. Took the dogs out for a walk, pootled about doing this and that.'

'And now you've gone back to bed.'

He ignored the comment and returned to the subject in hand.

'I don't think people will like the name. Goats smell.'

'So do mink, but that hasn't put people off wearing them,' I retorted.

'Yes, but mink are exotic and goats are just goats.'

'Mink bite, smell and scratch, and they kill indiscriminately. Don't you think Himalayan goats on snow-covered peaks are a bit more exotic?'

Robin was losing interest. I could hear him shuffling the Sunday papers.

'I just don't think single-word names carry much weight. The Pashmina Company has authority,' he countered.

'It worked for Chanel.'

'That's different.'

'Why?'

'Oh all right, I'll file it under Goat.' He paused for a moment. 'What about the Goat Company?'

A few minutes' walk from my flat is a very discreet, very smart health club where the glitterati and literati of Notting Hill go to hone and polish their bodies. Those who are quite famous make a lot of noise and talk loudly to each other across the walkers and the step machines about agents, contracts, bad performances (of others) and great performances (their own). They wear very new, very tight gym kit. The genuinely famous slip silently in and out. They wear old tracksuits and tired T-shirts, and they work out quietly with personal trainers, ignoring the fascinated sidelong glances of other gym-users.

The genuinely famous do not publicly carry mobile telephones. The quite famous carry them but make a show of turning them off when they go to work out. The not-famous-at-all leave theirs turned on, regardless of where they are. They need to talk all the time.

At the beginning of December I crept into the club at a quiet time of day to see if there were any part-time or off-peak rates. I explained that I was not in London that often. The manageress eyed the pashmina shawl that I was wearing. I could see her train of thought. Why would I need to get a cheap rate if I could afford a shawl that cost over £300?

'I didn't buy this here. I get them in India and import them,' I explained.

'How much do you sell them for?' she asked, and blinked when I told her.

'Would you like to have a sale of them here?'

'Yes, of course, as long as I can still join the club.'

She laughed. 'Being a salesman doesn't preclude you from membership.'

'I'll give you trade price on a shawl if you give me a better rate.'

'What's this, some kind of barter system?'

'Too much time spent haggling over the price of everything in India. I'm sorry, it's become a habit.'

'Well, I'm always hearing people talking about pashmina so I'm sure there will be a lot of interest. We'll put signs up around the place. You'll probably sell out, given the difference between what you're charging and the price at the clip-joint around the corner. Perhaps next week, to catch them all cashed-up for Christmas?'

Robin and I were very low on stock. The order that I had made several weeks earlier had still not materialized, though there had been many promises and references to Allah's will.

Manzoor was still in Srinagar with his children around him. Yaseen thought it more appropriate that I should call Manzoor. He did not have any news to give me but he did give me a number for the house by the lake in Kashmir.

I spent an hour trying to get through. Whoever it was who eventually answered the telephone did not understand what I was saying. I asked for Manzoor repeatedly until the voice at the other end disappeared. I heard footsteps clattering away across the room. I waited while the shadows of other international calls echoed down the line. Then I heard Manzoor crossing the room, shouting instructions as he came. '*Salaam alekum*, my friend. I am with my childrens at this time. Is it possible that you could be calling me back one hour from now?'

'Oh, I'm sorry, of course I will, but could you try and be close to a telephone then? It is very difficult to get through at the moment.'

But Manzoor had gone, leaving me to talk to the ghosts on the line.

When I got him an hour later he was in an ebullient mood.

'Let me tell you this, it is unbelievable here, you should be with us. We have the most beautiful of snow all over my valley. Me and my childrens have been talking of all things of snow and of Allah. My sons who are here with me from the school in your UK are so good. My number one son has fourteen of the thirty *suras* of the Koran by heart. It has taken him just two years to get to this level. It is taking most children of his age a great deal more of time. Do you not think this is unbelievable? Fourteen of our great *suras* marked on his heart for all time! I tell you this, I am almost to bursting with pride for this son of mine.'

'That is very good news but I rang about the last order that I made. I'm still waiting for it. When are you going to be able to send it to me?'

'What are you saying? It is not so good on this line. Perhaps it is okay if you call me one more time.'

'What about if you call me, Manzoor?' I shouted down the empty line.

As a Kashmiri, it was beneath Manzoor's dignity to call me back. As a woman in need of shawls I called him.

Once again we went through the greetings.

'Please, can you tell me when you are going to send me the last order of shawls? I have sales coming up and at the moment I have no shawls to sell. Manzoor, this is not good business.'

'Ah, my dear, this thing I have to explain to you. The most

incredible thing, more snow than we have been having in Kashmir for fifty years. You will not believe this but all of our rivers are flowing so fast on account of the snow, rushing, rushing into the lake, and so lake is all cloudy. We cannot wash shawls in the lake, it will make all your beautiful colours bad. What am I to do?'

'Do you mean you wash all the shawls in Dal Lake?'

The lake was dangerously polluted. There had been a time when it was not only safe to swim in it but it had been possible to dip a pot over the side of a boat and make *chai* straight from Dal water. Since then the lake had become more of a health risk. Now Manzoor was telling me that he washed all our shawl dyes into the same water.

'But of course. It is only way. Is Kashmir dyeing not best in India, if not whole world?' he asked.

'Yes it is, but the lake is already so polluted.' I stopped for a moment. 'Are the dyers using the same chemicals that Parveen uses in Delhi?'

'But of course, they are only using best of quality,' Manzoor replied proudly.

'Do you mean that you are just rinsing all those chemicals straight into the lake? What about the fish, the floating gardens, the lotuses and the lilies?' Dyed and dying.

There was silence from Manzoor.

'Can you hear me, Manzoor? Hello?'

The line had gone dead again.

I tried to get through for a further hour. In the end a sweet voice told me in Hindi and English that it was no longer possible to connect calls. So I rang Yaseen in Delhi instead to see if there was a fax number in Srinagar. There was.

Dear Manzoor
   It was good to speak to you today. However, I am concerned about the dyers rinsing our shawls in Dal Lake. In the West we have become very conscious of

Flower-seller and water-taxi of Nagin Lake

pollution. Industries here are now encouraged by the government to make the greatest efforts to avoid polluting rivers, lakes and the sea. Besides, Dal Lake and Nagin Lake are too beautiful to spoil. Is there no other way of rinsing the shawls?

I am sorry to keep interrupting your valuable time with your children but I do need to know when you will be sending me the shawls. My hope is that this business will continue to increase, but if there are always problems like this, it is going to be difficult to be successful.

There was a day's pause.

My dear
Salaams to you and your good family. Please be assured that we have your good wishes and needs close to our hearts at all times. You are surely knowing how

much we value to do business with you. We thank you for your kind considerations for our valley. It is a most difficult situation, this you must understand. Dyers of Kashmir have to make business so that they can feed their families. If they are not washing shawls in lake there is no place for washing. To buy the biggest of baths as you have seen at Parveen is most costly for local Kashmiris. It is very hard for my peoples. Please believe me when I tell you that I am looking most carefully into ways of rinsing. I am to talk to dyers on this very matter. On important matter of your shawls I have been consulting with the dyers even this morning, very first thing, even before greeting my childrens. I am telling them that you are most valuable customer. They are to make greatest efforts on your behalf. They have made big promise to me that they will have shawls ready for me in two days. I will send straight to Delhi and then another two days to you. So six days at most to your good door. You have my word on this, *inshallah*. Is this not good news?

It was too easy. The apparently insurmountable had been overcome in the curl of just one fax. The new stock was supposedly arriving on the same day as the first of the sales that I had arranged. I postponed all the sales by four days.

The shawls did arrive, three days later than Manzoor had promised. They were soft and delicate, but they smelt of the Kashmiri dyer's pot and they were virtually all the wrong colour.

Robin was agitated. 'What am I supposed to do?' he shouted down the telephone.

'Sell them!' I shouted back.

'But they are all the wrong colours.'

'We know that, but they don't. These were just the colours you and I picked. No one else will realize that. No one else has seen the colour charts.' I paused. 'Or have they, have you shown people the charts?'

'I suppose I might have mentioned them to one or two of the boutique brigade.'

'What do you mean, mention?'

'Oh all right, of course I bloody well showed them! How else were they supposed to choose the colours?'

'Did you leave the colour charts with them?' I asked.

'No.'

'Well, that's fine then, they will be getting variations on a theme that we will just have to hope they do not remember.'

'This is really bloody annoying!' Robin stormed.

'I know it is but if we continue to buy from village weavers and then insist on getting our shawls dyed in Kashmir during the worst winter in fifty years, this kind of thing is going to become the norm rather than an occasional irritation.'

'Not very professional,' Robin muttered.

'Neither are we.'

'What do you mean?' he bridled.

'Well, it's just us, my ansaphone and your unreliable fax machine. It's not exactly an empire, is it?'

'Branson started in a phone box,' said Robin, and he crashed down the receiver.

The day got worse. Brittle early December sun collapsed into heavy rain. I had to carry boxes and baskets of shawls to the smart health club for the sale. A deep moss green pashmina slid off the top of one of the boxes and out of its plastic bag. It flopped into a puddle and I watched as it turned almost black. The rain increased and I left the shawl in the puddle while I took the rest inside.

A girl with sculpted arms and a tattoo on her shoulder leant over the reception desk to see what was in the boxes.

'Are those them?' she asked. She seemed underwhelmed.

When I went back out to the puddle the sodden shawl had gone.

The manageress of the club was sympathetic over the loss as she showed me to the room where I was to have the sale – the members' lounge she called it. The green-tinted mirrors and low lighting were intended to relax but I found them disturbing. The length of one wall was glass, an underground window with fluid green light beyond. I started to lay out the shawls, trying to drape them fetchingly on unfetching furniture. They were all tinged green by the light. Peering through the window I was suddenly faced with a pair of naked legs dangling a few feet from me as a swimmer in the club pool took a pause before rising up out of view again.

I could do nothing about the light so I scuttled across the road to the café outside which, over a year before, I had made my first sale.

Tom's Deli was full of late-afternoon coffee drinkers who leant over tables, discussing things in low serious voices. I ordered coffee to take away and perched on a stool by the counter while I waited. Beside the nearest table stood a pram and a Moses basket. The two women at the table were quite unlike the rest of the clientele. They were frantically busy, exchanging news in high-pitched voices, drinking coffee and trying to eat between snatches of conversation and the demands of their children. One of them was bottle-feeding a baby in the Moses basket. The other was trying to stop her toddler from eating sugar-lumps out of a bowl on the table. When she took the bowl away he began to scream. She apologized to the café in general and stuck a sugar-lump in his mouth.

As I paid, the Moses basket mother reached over and stroked my dark lilac shawl.

'Is that pashmina?' she asked.

'Yes it is, pashmina and silk,' I replied.

'The stuff that I never stop hearing about at the moment?'

'Yes.'

She held my shawl up to her face.

'I've asked Harry to get me one for Christmas but to be honest I wasn't absolutely sure what it was.'

'Is Harry your husband?'

'Yes, Harry-not-a-clue. If I didn't tell him what to get he'd just go out and buy me another hot-water-bottle cover, bless him. Where did you get yours?' she asked.

'I live in India quite a lot of the time. I buy them there and sell quite a few of them here.'

'How wonderful, can I send Harry to you?' She clapped her hands.

Everyone in the café was watching.

'Yes, of course. I'm actually about to have a sale just across the road at the health club if you want to come along.'

'Oh, Harry will be so pleased. He won't have to go anywhere near Bond Street. He's going to love me. We'll see you there then.'

Paper coffee cup in hand, I trotted back to the club through the rain. Already there were several women shuffling through the shawls in the green light, and several pairs of legs dangling behind them in the watery window.

'Could I take this up to the ladies' changing-room?' asked one woman as she headed for the door with a shawl. 'At least there's proper light up there. I really can't tell what colour this is down here.'

She did not wait for my reply.

I knew the shawl was a dark turquoise that would wash her out. I shrugged as others followed her and tried to count them out of the door while wrapping, writing out invoices and answering questions. More people arrived.

'Do you take credit cards?'

'No, I'm sorry, I don't,' I replied to a tall Frenchwoman.

'Well, then, I cannot buy these.'

She had four shawls draped over her arm.

'I am sorry, but I'm afraid I don't have one of those machines.'

She swore and dropped the shawls at my feet.

The two mothers from the café were happily writing cheques.

'Oh dear, very French,' whispered the mother with the Moses basket as she signed. She was now the owner of one baby blue shawl and one baby pink shawl.

At intervals the changing-room colour-testers came back down, voluble about the colour difference caused by the light, less loud about paying for their goods.

A man wearing a banana cycling helmet strode in. He put down his backpack and took off his wet coat. I winced as he dropped it on top of a pile of shawls. He left his helmet in place, the chin-strap tightly fastened beneath a stubbly chin. He did not look like a promising customer.

'Right now, can't be long. I've heard all about these so I'm going to do all my Christmas shopping in one go. I need one for my assistant, one for my secretary, one for the girlfriend and one for my mother.'

'Will your girlfriend mind getting the same thing as your assistant and your secretary?' I asked. I was learning fast.

'Good point. Better make it two each for Mother and the girlfriend. You choose the colours. So what does that come to? Company cheque okay?'

'Absolutely fine, thanks.'

I tried to colour-match his various women as he tried to remember the colour of their hair and eyes. I wrapped and he wrote out a cheque. He stuffed the packages into his backpack, donned his coat and then, surprisingly, kissed me on the cheek, his helmet rather spoiling the effect by catching me full on the temple. The whole thing had taken about four minutes, my best sale to date.

The coffee from the café sat undrunk in a corner, the room was littered with rumpled shawls, there was a queue of women waiting to pay and still there were two hours of the sale to go.

A tall black girl swayed into the room, swing-hipped, loose-limbed and beautiful.

'Hi,' she said in a low, sexy voice.

My best customer in the banana helmet stood rooted to the spot as she passed, her grey jersey dress riding every long fine muscle of her body.

'I heard about your shawls, so here I am.'

She picked up a coral-coloured one.

'This one is so pretty. How does it look?' she asked, holding it against her face.

'Wonderful, you look wonderful,' said the banana helmet from the door before I had a chance to reply.

'Thank you, that is kind.' She smiled back at him.

He melted.

She had side-tracked us with her sinuous charm. But while the cycling helmet and I were enjoying the diversion, the rest of the ladies queuing up were becoming impatient. I went back to the invoice book and the tissue paper. When I next looked up the tall black girl had wrapped herself in coral and was patiently waiting for me to finish. I wrote out an invoice for her.

'Someone told me that you do this to help out kids in the slums,' she said.

I told her about the schools.

'It must give you so much pleasure.' Her smile was easy and open.

'Yes, it does.'

'Thank you, I'm going to enjoy this.' She picked up her package and invoice, waving as she left. Another perfect customer.

A woman in a long loden coat had been standing watching the performance. She was holding a shawl over her arm.

'How much is this?' she asked.

There was a large sign on the table listing the prices. She must have seen it. I repeated them. She narrowed her eyes and said nothing but continued to stand over me as I sold to someone else.

'They seem quite expensive to me, ' she said after a pause.

'At the moment they are a great deal cheaper than anywhere else around here,' I replied.

'Are you really supporting slum schools?'

'Yes.'

'I've heard so many of these kinds of stories. Do you mean to tell me that all you lot who ship stuff over from India and then whack up the price are really putting money into all these worthy causes? Or are you all just having a jolly good tug at our heart-strings?'

'I can't speak for other sellers but yes, this does help schools in some of Delhi's slum areas.'

'Do you make any money out it yourself?' she asked.

'No, not at the moment.'

'Well, why are you doing it then?' she pushed.

'I'm sorry, I'd like to be able to tell you a lot more about the project but I'm a bit short-handed here.'

'Fine, I won't have this one then, I'll shop around.' She held the shawl out to me.

'Fine.' I cleared my throat, held on to my patience and turned to another customer.

'No need to be rude,' she muttered, rebuttoning her coat very precisely.

I looked up at her from my place on the floor and smiled. She pursed her small mouth and left.

'BSE,' said a pretty girl with pale blonde hair.

'What?' I asked.

'Mad cow.'

'She didn't like me,' I said.

'No, she probably doesn't like much,' said the girl as she wrote out a cheque. Her accent was soft Long Island and Maine beach holidays.

'You only bought two shawls, this is for three,' I told her when she handed me the cheque.

'I know, but there's a bit more for the schools.'

'Thank you, that's a very generous thing to do.'

'Anyone can write a cheque, there's nothing very heroic about that. Anyway, I still got two shawls for the price of half of one that I was looking at yesterday.' She smiled again and slipped away.

The last hour was quieter. Notting Hill was beginning to wake up for the evening. The first rush of pashmina bargain-hunters were now wrapped in their new buys, parading them in local restaurants, bars and cafés. I had sold fifty shawls in two and a half hours. Company profits had doubled.

The manageress came in as I was packing away what was left. She picked up a cream shawl.

'This is pretty.' She stroked it against her face.

'It's for you,' I said.

'Oh I know, I love cream, but I haven't got any money at the moment.' She began to fold it up.

'No, I mean I want you to have it,' I explained.

'You're joking.' She held it out in front of her.

'You let me have the sale here. Please take it,' I said.

She helped me carry the boxes and baskets back out to my car.

'You must come and do another one,' she said, holding a fitness magazine over her head to keep off the rain.

'Thank you, perhaps when I next come back from India with a new batch.'

'Perfect, and don't forget to fill in your membership form.' She waved as I drove away.

It was still raining when I went back to Tom's Deli the following afternoon, this time to sit and drink coffee and try to balance the invoice books from the sale. There was a spare table in the corner. At two of the other tables were women who had been at the sale. They were both wearing their shawls and they both ignored me and each other.

As I waited for coffee a pale blonde head ducked down in front of me. It was the girl from the sale at the club who had overpaid for her two shawls. She too was wearing one of her new purchases.

'Look, I love it! I haven't taken it off since yesterday. My husband says I've become like Linus with his blanket. They're some of the most beautiful things I have ever had. Thank you.' She smiled and looked around the café. There were no spare tables.

'Please, sit here if you don't mind sharing,' I said.

'Do you mind?'

'Of course not.'

'Are you sure you're English?' she laughed.

'All of me, except the bits that get left behind in India.'

'There you go. That makes you hardly English at all. Being asked to join someone at a table in Tom's, in Notting Hill? I don't think so.' She perched on the chair opposite me, her back very straight, her legs wound tightly in a double cross.

A waitress came over.

'Could I have a skinny decaf cappuccino, please?' Her tone was almost apologetic. 'You can get the girl out of New York but you can never quite get the New York coffee ordering out of the girl,' she explained, and smiled.

We drank coffee and she told me her only Kashmiri story. She had been caught smoking one of her father's hand-rolled Turkish cigarettes when she was fifteen by her mother. Then she had thrown up all over her mother's beloved Kashmiri silk carpet in the sitting-room of their New York brownstone. She had been grounded for a month. She was funny and easy to talk to, and she insisted on paying for my cup of coffee.

We left the café together.

'Do you remember the mad cow woman yesterday?' she asked, as we walked back out into the rain.

'Yes.'

'I think it was so disgusting what she said. My husband asked me about where the profits go last night and I didn't really know any more than what you said to her about the slum schools. Can you tell me a bit more?'

I began the story about Gautam, DRAG and the schools. We stopped under a bus shelter outside the café. She upended one of the plastic seats and sat down next to a large Jamaican woman who was knitting what appeared to be a purple windsock. It was not really the weather to be out with your knitting but the woman seemed quite happy. I became involved in my story. A bus came and went and the knitter continued to sit and listen. The pretty blonde was a perfect audience. As I described one of the schools where I knew most of the children, she put out her hand to stop me.

'Tell me about one of them, tell me his or her name.'

I paused and then began to tell her about Rahul.

'He is six now. When I saw him for the first time at the school he used to sit in one corner on his own, rocking backwards and forwards. Well, corner is not actually accurate as the classes are held under a tree. He always kept just that distance away from the other children.'

'Did you notice him for any other reason?' she asked.

'Yes, he had blue eyes. That's unusual around Delhi.'

'Blue eyes?'

'He comes from your favourite carpet spot. Some Kashmiris have blue eyes. His parents are Hindus, that's unusual as well. They were burnt out of their home in Srinagar in 1991 when the situation up there was bad. They've been in the Delhi slum ever since.

'For a long time Rahul wouldn't join in the class but just sat doing his rocking thing. Then before the Diwali festival this year the children were making cards, and he decided to have a go too. He laughed when he saw how the crayons turned the paper different colours. He thought it was magic. No one had heard Rahul laugh before. I don't think he had heard himself laugh very much

The slum school under a tree

either. He kept putting his hand in front of his mouth, almost as if he was frightened about letting out the sound. He looked beautiful.'

As I finished, the Jamaican woman put down her knitting and clapped. Gautam would have smiled.

CHAPTER 6

A Wangnoo
in London

MANZOOR RANG ME a couple of days after the health-club sale and left a message on my ansaphone.

'*Salaam alekum.* Are you hearing this message? I am in your country bringing my childrens back to school. I am in Dewsbury, close by to Manchester. I am having some good news for you and some other news. I have no knowledge of telephone number here. I will have to be calling you back on this matter.'

I didn't like the sound of 'other' news.

He rang again a few days later. This time I was in.

'Manzoor, it's lovely to hear your voice but I don't understand why you are in England.'

'My childrens are wanting me to see their college and I am having business here in Dewsbury, and in Leicester too.' He pronounced Leicester as if it was an exotic disease. 'But I am having most wonderful news for you. We have found weaver for one hundred per cent pashmina. I tell you it is unbelievable, my dear, most beautiful thing you have seen in your life.'

'That sounds good, although you know that I need more of the pashmina silk mix at the moment. And what about the other news?' I asked.

'Ah, this I cannot be telling to you on telephone. I am to come from Dewsbury day after for business in London. Can we make meeting?'

'You could come to my house,' I suggested without thinking. 'I assume you'll arrive by train. My house is not very far from King's Cross.'

'It is not possible for me to come to your house. It is not allowed.' He sounded offended.

'Of course, I'm sorry.' It would be unacceptable for a Muslim man like Manzoor to go into a single woman's home. I should have remembered.

'We could meet at my club,' I suggested.

'What kind of place is it?' he asked.

'Well, it's a club where people go to talk, to have meetings . . .' Manzoor cut in before I had time to finish.

'It is place where peoples are drinking and ladies are showing themselves. This is a place I cannot go to.' His tone was strident.

'No, Manzoor, it is not like that at all. We can meet there in the afternoon and have tea. I have a lot of my meetings there. It is very quiet in the afternoon, perhaps just a couple of other people having Earl Grey and sandwiches.' I began to have doubts even as I spoke.

'Will Kashmiri Muslim be allowed to enter?' he asked.

'We're more accepting in England now than we used to be.'

'What is this meaning?'

I stopped. Again I wasn't sure. If Manzoor turned up at a club in Chelsea in his *feron*, *topi* and full beard, would he be allowed in without question or would he be quizzed about who he intended to meet or asked if he had the correct address? I didn't know.

'What I meant was I think you will find that people are not so quick to judge here as they sometimes are in India.' I spoke with more confidence than I felt.

'This is good thing. I am feeling fine about this thing. I am happy to be meeting you at your club.'

We arranged a time and I gave him elaborate directions, aware, even as I described the streets, that he was neither writing anything down nor really listening. After the phonecall I thought about his concern that he might not be admitted. Perhaps I should ring the club and check.

'But, madam, of course we will welcome your colleague. It will be a pleasure for us,' said the polite manager.

'And you really don't think that there will be any problem?' I pressed.

'Madam, please be assured that we have members of every race and religious belief. Any guest of yours is welcome in the club. We are confident that you would not bring anyone in who would make any of the other guests feel uncomfortable.' There was a code, a standard of behaviour, and my side of the bargain was to judge what would or would not make other members feel uncomfortable.

I arrived an hour early on the day of my meeting with Manzoor just in case he had got the time wrong, though it was unlikely because the Wangnoos generally ran about two hours late for most things except prayer. For half an hour I was the only person in the club. The barman made me a cup of coffee behind the long chrome bar, the sound of the steam jet in the milk loud in the silence. His movements were controlled, an Edward Hopper painting in motion. The silence returned, discreet and upholstered. There was just the sound of other waiters crossing the marble hallway behind the seal of the rosewood and glass door.

Two men broke the vacuum. They had come down from the club dining-room after what had obviously been an over-extended lunch. They were drunk and one of them was obviously finding it difficult to focus as he slewed towards the bar. The barman gently diverted him away from where I was sitting and towards a sofa along the wall. 'Excuse me, sir, I think you will find this more comfortable.'

I looked nervously towards the door, conscious that fate would probably bring in teetotal Manzoor just at this particular moment.

I needn't have worried. The time of our appointment came and went. I sat watching the door and listening to the conversations around me as the room filled up. Manzoor was now an hour late, then two. I gave up waiting and went home.

It took him another three days to ring and explain his absence. He was still in Dewsbury with his children. Great Northeastern Railways had failed him repeatedly, he assured me. He insisted that Indian Railways were much more reliable. He would absolutely be in London by the end of the week.

'It is most vital that we are meeting before we two are returning to Delhi. I have such things to discuss with you, unbelievable things.'

By the time he had managed to acquire a rail ticket and passage from the Greater Manchester area to Southall it was only a week before I was due to return to Delhi.

'You will come to the place where I am,' he announced. 'This will be seeming much better to me, and for you too I am thinking.'

A journey to Southall was not what I had in mind amidst the packing, mail redirection, homeopathic anti-malarial treatments and writing deadlines that hovered on the edge of every sleepless night.

'Yes, Manzoor, of course.'

A series of cousins were then put on the line to give me directions to where I was going. All of them centred around the Bengali Spice Market in the middle of Southall. It was not marked on the map. Neither was I confident about being directed to turn left or right at certain bus stops and *halal* meat vendors. When the third cousin came on the line, I finally got a street name and number, something I could apply to the A *to* Z.

It was raining as I drove the length of drab, grey Uxbridge Road but as I approached Southall, the scenery changed. Suddenly there were saris and *salwar kameez* everywhere I looked, and

Indian shops full of tins of *paneer*, the ubiquitous Indian cottage cheese, sacks of dried green and red chillies, jars of Indian sweets past their sell-by-date, and boxes of spangled *bindi* marks, jazzed-up forehead dots for the modern Indian-English women of Southall. Among the saris and *salwar kameez* were small groups of girls in mini-skirts and high heels, some pushing prams, some huddling into their leather jackets. Their cold bare legs looked as incongruous as Southall Council's Christmas lights – giant candles suspended from wires across the street.

I turned left at the *halal* butcher and right at the bus stop, as instructed.

The door was answered by one of Manzoor's cousins, a young man in white *feron* and *topi,* the first wisps of a beard sketched on his chin, his thick, dark hair cropped close to his neck under his cap. He bowed low and then stood up very straight to shake my hand with a persistent pumping action.

'*Salaam alekum*, you are most welcome.' He held out his hand, the fingers long and elegant, to indicate where I should go, along the corridor with its peeling formica'd walls to the door at the end.

On the door was a poster showing the four pillars of Islam. In the first scene a *feron-* and *topi-*wearing Kashmiri was in the act of *salut*, prayer. In the next, he was doling out *zakat*, coins to the poor, along a road that looked like so many of the roads that lead out of Srinagar, long, straight and lined with *chinar* trees. The third showed our Kashmiri hero looking hollow-cheeked and hungry – the Fast. In the last he was on *haj*, the pilgrimage to Mecca, the minarets of the city shimmering in the distance. The wispily bearded young man seemed pleased that I had paused to take in the scenes and ushered me on with a smile.

'You are liking the art of Islam?'

'Yes, it's very interesting.'

'You are reading the *suras*?'

'I'm trying to.'

He gave me an indulgent smile, one from the man he would become.

'Uncle is waiting, come.'

Manzoor was sitting among his cousins looking thoroughly at home. The National Cottage Emporium had been transported to a Southall kitchen-cum-diner. The cooking area had been curtained off with a fall of Kashmiri crewel-work, chain-stitched flowers tumbling in cascades amidst maple leaves and vines. Where, in a Western household, there might have been a table, a sofa, a television, a CD player, there were large flat cushions laid out on top of a series of carpets, the patterns and colours familiar from the stacks I had seen in the Wangnoo godown in Surjan Singh Park. Among the cushions was a lacquered papier-mâché tray showing the standard Mogul polo scene, twiglet-legged ponies leaping under bearded, heavily robed riders. And on the tray were all the ingredients of Kashmiri *kawa* tea. The scent of cardamom, cinnamon bark, cloves and saffron filled the room at 43 St John's Street, Southall.

Manzoor sat among his own, each one of them a reflection of the other, seniority revealed in the grey hairs in their beards, one older man with his hair hennaed, marking him as a *hajji*, a pilgrim of Mecca.

Manzoor reached out his hand, waving for me to join them. I hung back in the doorway. There were no other women in the room, though the sound of female voices could be heard from behind the crewel curtain.

'Hello, my friend.' Manzoor was safe in his surroundings. He sounded much more relaxed than he had when he was being challenged by the vicissitudes of Great Northeastern Railways.

I sat among his cousins and listened to stories of the boom days in Kashmir during the eighties when the travellers and tourists came weighed down with City bonuses, when Manzoor had been making so much money that he had been able to fly the whole family over to see the college near Manchester, to plan the future education of his children.

'Let me tell you this.' Manzoor replaced his cup on the tray to mark the beginning of his speech.

'I am having young man coming into my shop in Srinagar. In this city of yours you would be calling him beggar. His clothes were like rag-picker in Delhi. So I am thinking to myself how to get this person out of my shop and I am saying this to my brothers. This is for reason that we are many times having raggy-taggy peoples coming into our shops, hippie tourists who are asking to see carpets, sitting down all over my cushions in their clothes that have not seen *dhobi* for many months. And we are just giving them tea and more tea and they are just sitting, sitting and never buying. So this man looking like other raggy-taggys is making me and my brothers think that he will be same. Then I am thinking of Koran and how we are told to make all men who come to our house as our brothers. So I am not asking this man to leave but making him feel most comfortable with tea. I am saying to him that he is most welcome in my shop and that we are happy for him to be with us. Is this not good?'

The uncles, cousins and I all nodded our heads.

Manzoor rolled on.

'And I am right in this thing, for as soon as we are drinking tea he is telling me he is wanting to see carpets. And do you know what is in my mind?'

The uncles, cousins and I all shook our heads.

'I am thinking this is just young man doing this thing to have as many cups of *kawa* tea as it is possible for him to take. But I am giving him my time and showing him carpets, and he is looking all the time and asking me questions that make me believe that he is knowing something of carpets. He is knowing about the numbers of knots and the quality of silk. He is knowing how to test for silk carpet and to take sample on razor from across whole of carpet so he cannot be fooled by carpets with just some silk on the outside. He is razoring from my carpets and burning what he cuts. He is happy it is all silk and I am not putting wool in and telling lies to him.'

Manzoor turned to me.

'You know about this?' he asked.

I nodded. I had seen his brother Ashraf doing the same thing many times for customers. He would flourish a razor blade across a wide section of a silk carpet, shaving away some of the surface. Then he would burn it. Silk does not burn, it smoulders. Wool burns with the acrid smell of human hair.

'So I am telling you, this young man is only son of biggest store-owner in New York in United States. His father is asking him to find new carpet supplier. Young man is working for his father finding good sources of best-quality goods. I am not lying to you. This was because of Allah and the words of Koran that are making me and my brothers polite towards this young man. After we are making business, young man is telling to me that he is making choice of National Cottage Emporium because of how welcome we are making him. He is saying to me that many of the other carpet-sellers are turning him away because they are not believing that he has business. It was Will of God, for I am not understanding about how young peoples are dressing, looking to me like rag-pickers.' Manzoor raised his hands and we sat for a moment in reverential silence.

'What does pashmina smell like when it burns?' I asked.

Manzoor gave me a long look. 'Ah, I see you are wanting to talk business. Is it not great news that we have found supplier of one hundred per cent pashmina?'

'Yes, I am delighted, but you did say that there was some other news as well,' I replied.

'This is very bad thing that I am to tell you of. For this reason I had to be face for face with you. It is better this way than to be talking on telephone.' Manzoor sighed, resettled himself on his cushion and then dropped his bombshell. 'All of stock in Delhi is gone.'

'What do you mean?' I asked.

'Someone from Japan is coming to Delhi and putting advertisement in paper saying that best prices will be paid by him for all stocks of pashmina mixed with silk. All of drivers leaving from Srinagar with lorries all full of pashmina silk are hearing this and taking shawls to this man. We have nothing at this time of pashmina silk. It is most terrible thing.' He put his head in his hands and rubbed his forehead against his palms.

'I'm sorry, Manzoor, I'm not sure that I really understand,' I said.

'We have no pashmina silk shawls,' he intoned.

'No shawls?'

'Not one piece.'

'What can we do?' I begged.

'*Inshallah*, we will be finding answers to this. I am having all of my boys working on this thing. I am sending peoples to Kathmandu to seek for shawls.' Manzoor was looking down at the cushions.

'But I thought you told me that pashmina silk from Nepal was not nearly such good quality as the Kashmiri stock.'

'This is so.' Manzoor shook his head.

'But I have sold shawls to people sight unseen on the proviso that they will be the same quality as the ones that I have had until now. I will lose business. Manzoor, these people do not understand the vagaries of India.'

'What is proviso and vagaries?' he asked.

'What I am saying is that I have made promises to people and I cannot expect them to buy from me if I offer them something that is not the same quality. In Europe and America this is not acceptable. Buyers are not interested in the reasons why. There is only one thing that they care about and that is the result, the consistent quality of the product. If I cannot give them the same product every time, they will not want to buy.' I took a deep breath.

Manzoor rubbed his head in his hands again.

'I am thinking that maybe this is not a place that I am wanting to do business.' He reached towards the pot of tea and stopped just as he was about to pour. 'You must understand that the things

A Kashmiri pashmina handloom

I am doing is for my childrens. They are asking me for things. What am I to do? As a father it is my duty to provide.' He poured the tea.

'What does it say in the Koran?' I asked.

Manzoor looked at me with a disgusted expression.

'What is this you are asking me?' His voice was very quiet.

'I'm sorry, I did not mean to be offensive. I was just wondering what the Koran said about children and a parent's duty.'

'I cannot speak of these things now. We are to be leaving. I am staying in your London proper. I have meeting there soon. You are driving me?' Manzoor got up, nodding to his relations.

'I'm not sure I understand. You asked me to come out here and now you want me to take you back into London. Why did I come all the way out here if you are staying in central London?'

'It was important to me for you to be meeting with my uncles and cousins. They were all asking me that they could meet with you.'

I had not exchanged a single word with any of Manzoor's relations except the young man who had opened the door.

'Come, now we must go.' Manzoor pointed towards the hall.

I nodded my greetings and my goodbyes to the assembled group.

'Now this thing is done, it is needful that we are driving with haste. The time of my meeting is soon.'

Manzoor folded himself and a very efficient-looking briefcase into my small car, a plastic bag full of documents held over his head by one of the younger cousins to shelter him from the rain. Another cousin loaded a vast suitcase into the boot and then filled the back seat with several smaller ones.

'You are knowing how to get to this place, Sheraton Park Towers?' Manzoor asked.

I stopped with my hand on the ignition key while the information that Manzoor was staying in one of the most expensive hotels in London sank in.

'Why are you staying there?' I asked.

'Because of having many meetings with Harrods. Carpet-buyer has to come to see what I am having. Sheraton is close by to Harrods.'

'I suppose so but it is terribly expensive.' I tried not to sound surprised that Manzoor was staying in a five-star hotel in Knightsbridge. He would be lolloping along the pavements outside the very shops where his shawls, dyed in Kashmir and rinsed in Dal Lake, ended up with price tags in steep multiples of their real worth. His *feron* would be brushing against the shawls that he had bundled up in calico, now draped over the shoulders of women rushing for cappuccinos, facials and hair appointments.

'While I was staying with my good friend Habib in Dewsbury he was taking me to see some of his very good customers. I am telling you this, my dear, these are peoples with very much money. I am not believing that they can be living in houses so big.' He stretched his hands wide to indicate the enormity of the wealth he was talking about. His fingers waved in my face. I swerved.

'Careful how you are driving, this is most important meeting for me.' He clutched the dashboard. 'These houses I am speaking about, they are having just two peoples living in them. Can you believe this thing? Such big houses for just two peoples. In Srinagar, I am having a house of some size, not as big in any way as the houses of which I am speaking, but my house is full of peoples and childrens all the time. Me, my brothers, all our childrens, thirteen childrens running about my house at all times. Just two people, unbelievable!'

'People in Delhi live in big houses,' I countered.

'This is true, but they are living there with their families and childrens. Just two peoples!' He shook his head in disbelief.

As we came into Knightsbridge, Manzoor began to get agitated. He snapped his briefcase open and shut, trapping his fingers and muttering in Kashmiri.

'Would you like me to drop you at Harrods or at the Sheraton?'

'Hotel, this is place for meeting.' He was abrupt.

'I would like to have more of a meeting at some point, please,' I said. 'We really didn't achieve very much today, although of course it was a great pleasure to meet your relations.'

'Come tomorrow to hotel.'

It was an order.

'Okay.'

We set a time and then he jumped out of the car the second I drew up outside the hotel. He strode into the building, his brief-case in one hand, the other running through his beard. I waited. He reappeared through the revolving doors, trotted back to the car and tapped on the window.

'Your luggage?' I asked.

'Of course,' he said. 'Soon I will be losing this', he tapped his head, 'down through my trousers. Is this not so?' He smiled.

'I'll get a porter to bring it for you,' I offered.

Manzoor bowed and trotted back through the revolving doors, flipping the back of his *feron* free before it got caught in the twirl of glass.

My memory of him from Delhi was of a much taller man. I had always seen him in tight, crowded places. Now, in London, against the front of the Sheraton, he looked so small.

He rang me the following day, half an hour before I was due to meet him.

'Where are you?' he asked.

'I'm on my way to see you,' I replied.

'Good, very good. I have to check out of hotel at one-thirty, so it is good thing if we are meeting in lobby.'

'That sounds fine.'

Manzoor was sitting neatly at a table in the big lobby, his hands folded in his lap, his feet crossed at the ankle. He looked almost relieved to see me and shook my hand with both of his.

'Now, my dear, we can talk business in proper way.'

I sat down opposite him.

'How was the meeting with Harrods?' I asked.

'Unbelievable, almost unbelievable. I am now in Harrods, Wangnoo Brothers are selling in Harrods. Buyer was here with me for total of five hours. He could not believe what things I had brought for him from Kashmir. In Harrods, I am telling you, they have no good stuff. Harrods, greatest shop in whole of world and most terrible carpets.' Manzoor held the sides of his head. 'But this place, how to live here?'

'What do you mean?' I asked.

'You are having to do all of things yourself. What is this? I am having to unroll carpets, roll up carpets all by myself. This thing I am never doing in Delhi and Kashmir. And all of people rushing about all the time. Not one person has time for anything. Life in India is good, always peoples around to be doing things for you. In Dewsbury, Habib was asking me to make tea.' Manzoor was shocked.

I smiled. 'I am afraid that I have my car on a parking-meter and I do not have that much time,' I said.

'You see, you see what I am saying! Nothing of time, always rushing. Come, let us go inside.' He waved to one of the porters for his bags and we made a procession to the tea room: Manzoor and his briefcase, me with my various bits and pieces and one of Manzoor's smaller bags on wheels, the porter with Manzoor's huge suitcase, also on wheels, and several other smaller ones. We settled ourselves at another table.

'What is your wish?' he asked.

'No, you are in my town now, what would you like?' I asked.

'Tea.'

A waiter approached.

'We are having Earl Grey with all of the things,' Manzoor ordered. 'Now, I am showing you something beautiful.'

He dived into one of the suitcases and pulled out a pile of plastic bags. He rustled amongst them and out came a pale brown one hundred per cent pashmina. It bristled and puffed with static before settling across my knee. Only then was I able to see the paisley embroidery in pale lavender, the stitching sheer against the wool.

'How beautiful is this?' he asked.

'It's lovely. How much is it?'

Manzoor paused for a second before naming a huge figure.

'Please, I know we are in London but I can't pay you London shop prices. What would you ask me for it in Delhi?'

He shrugged and pulled the shawl gently away from my knees, flicking it over the back of the chair next to me so that I could look at it in its full glory as we talked.

We moved on to the new stock of pashmina mixed with silk that Manzoor had found despite the Japanese piracy and his claim that there had been not one pashmina silk shawl in the whole of Delhi. The piles of shawls mounted up around us. The waiter returned with his tea trolley. He tried to push the piles to one side. Manzoor waved him away and restacked the shawls under our chairs. He was silent while he watched the waiter pour the tea.

'Sugar? White, brown or sweetener?' asked the waiter.

Manzoor looked surprised. He wanted me to choose.

'Full milk, skimmed, or lemon?' the waiter continued.

Manzoor listened.

'Lemon and white sugar, please,' he decided.

He waited until the ceremony was over and the trolley had been wheeled away before turning to me. 'I am finding this very hard place. No one is caring for anyone else. See, even you are much more hard here, always in so much of hurry. No time for anything. This is not a good way to be living.' He smoothed out the lavender-embroidered shawl on the back of the chair.

'I don't stop to think about it too much. I suppose I live two lives really, my life here in a higher gear than my life in Delhi.'

129

'What is this about gears? We are not cars. Now, put this on just for two minutes to feel what it is like. Unbelievable, like wearing air, beautiful warm summer air from my valley.' He held the shawl out to me.

A woman in a pair of lilac suede trousers and matching stiletto boots sitting nearby watched closely as I took the shawl from Manzoor again. I did not want to try it on. I knew that once I did I would want to buy it. The woman waited and watched, smoothing her hands down her suede-covered thighs. I tried the shawl and, as I did, she narrowed her eyes. When a man sat down beside her, she whispered in his ear.

I agreed to buy the shawl and to pay Manzoor in cash for it and two hundred pashmina and silk shawls that he had promised me he would be able to secure in spite of the pashmina famine in Delhi. The subject of money made him speak very quickly and quietly.

'When can I have the money?' he asked.

'It's quite a lot. I'm not sure if I can just get it straight from the bank without clearing it through our account manager. It will probably take a few days to arrange,' I explained.

'So day after then?' he pressed.

'No, not that quickly. It will take a few days for me to get authorization. I will have to talk to my partner Robin as well, to make sure that he is happy about it.'

Manzoor continued to press me but the time on my parking meter was about to expire and I had to go. I took the bill, paid, folded my new shawl in a tiny bundle, wrapped it in tissue paper and put it into my handbag, thanked Manzoor and assured him that he could call me the next day and we would confirm when I could pay him. I could see him in a large mirror as I walked away. He was fussing among his plastic bags and the waiter was trying to tidy him away. Manzoor was not comfortable in London.

A young embroiderer working on a test shawl for Manzoor in Srinagar

It was getting dark as I left. It had been raining again and the roads and pavements reflected back passing car lights. High heels, sensible pumps, striding brogues and pumped-up trainers flapped past, escaping from the rain. Footwear was the only thing I could see under the rim of my umbrella. As I waited to cross the road, a pair of lilac stiletto boots flashed past and disappeared into the back of a long, low car. I reached out to open my own car door and a hand settled on my shoulder.

'I'm sorry to trouble you.' The hand and voice were those of the lilac-booted woman's companion from the hotel.

'My employer has asked me to speak with you.'

So not a companion, a bodyguard, tall, dark, heavy-lidded, black-suited, perhaps Lebanese or Iranian.

'How can I help you?' I asked nervously. I looked around to see if anyone was within shouting distance but the rain had emptied the street.

'The shawl that you just took from the Arab in the hotel, she would like to buy it.'

'He's a Kashmiri not an Arab, and I have only just bought it. I'm not sure I want to sell it yet,' I replied.

He ignored my reply. 'She says she would like to know how much you would charge.' His hand was still on my shoulder.

I stepped away to break the contact. As I moved back, he came towards me, pushing me up against the railings that lined the street.

'My employer is aware that it is a valuable piece and she is prepared to pay well for a ring-shawl.'

So, she had thought the shawl was a *shatoosh*. I was about to explain that it was not what she had thought, not a true ring-shawl. But of course it was a ring-shawl – one hundred per cent pashmina flies through a ring with the same liquid flow as *shatoosh*.

'Where is your employer?' I asked. 'I would like to talk to her.'

'She requested me to complete the transaction on her behalf.'

'I am not a drug-pusher and I do not enjoy being pinned against these railings. I would appreciate it if you would go to your employer and find out exactly how much she would like to pay for my ring-shawl, bearing in mind that I do not really have any intention of selling it. I would also like you to tell her that I would prefer to speak to her directly.' I sounded more confident than I felt.

'I am sorry, I did not mean to cause offence of any kind. Please accept my apology.' He stepped away. 'I will go and speak with my employer. You will wait here.' Once again, it was a command rather than a request.

'I will wait in my car.' I opened the door and got in, only then aware that I was wet from the rain. I had closed my umbrella as he had pounced.

I watched him walk back to the low-slung car. My instinct was to drive away but I was curious. Who was his employer and why couldn't she talk to me herself?

Before I had made up my mind what to do the man returned. 'She asks if you would like to come to the house.' He now carried a large umbrella. 'It is not far from here. Do you know Eaton Square?'

'Yes, thank you, I do.' Curiosity had won. 'Are you going to give me the address or shall I follow you?'

He gave me the number but I decided to follow the car anyway so that I could watch them arrive and make a final decision as to whether I should stay or run. I sat behind them at a set of traffic lights and looked at my reflection in their blackened windows. The car had a Saudi number plate. It turned right into the still, stuccoed enclave of the square. Polished pavements were reflected in glassy doors. The car stopped outside a door that had only one bell – a whole house, undivided. A chauffeur appeared and released the woman from the back of the car. Her bodyguard jumped out and opened his big black umbrella. The woman unfurled herself from the seat. At the hotel I had only noticed that she wore lilac and heels. I had an image of her watching as Manzoor and I negotiated. Now, as she stood in front of me on the pavement, she seemed taller and thinner than I had remembered, with long fine legs, a tiny clutch bag in one hand, a cashmere jersey wound around her like a dancer's warmer, a couple of inches of midriff on show, smooth and pale.

She did not acknowledge my car hovering beside her in the street but walked straight up to the house and disappeared inside as the chauffeur drove off.

As I started my car and began to pull away, an umbrella handle cracked against the window and the bodyguard's face came out of the dark. He pointed to the front door and indicated that I should open the window.

'You are leaving?' he asked.

'No, I was going to park,' I lied.

'She is waiting for you in the house.'

'Thank you,' I snapped, beginning to feel both uncomfortable and irritated. I got out and slammed the car door shut. The bodyguard smiled but did not hold his umbrella up for me.

I crossed the road behind him and waited for the door to open as it had for the mistress of the house. A small woman in a black dress and white apron let us in and muttered something to the bodyguard.

Madam was on the telephone to New York. A very important call, I was informed. I was to wait. I was taken to a side room off the marbled hall. The room was clad in seal-grey leather, the sofa, the chairs, a low table, even the walls. I turned to the bodyguard to see what my next instructions might be, if I would be told where to sit, but he had gone. I looked around. The expanses of leather made me feel nervous again. I perched on the edge of the sofa with my handbag between my feet. The shawl was tightly rolled up in the bottom, wrapped in tissue paper, everything else packed in on top to camouflage it. I did feel like a drug-pusher.

Then the door opened.

'I am so very sorry, this is very rude of me. My name is Alessandra, hello. Please, sit down.'

I had jumped up as she came in. I shook her outstretched hand and reassessed her. In the distance, in the hotel and then in the rain, I had assumed that she would have a hard edge to her, a brittle veneer. I was wrong. Alessandra was Italian and about twenty-five, and she had the face of an angel.

'My husband called. I have to take his calls, he does not like to have to call back. He is working very hard on a big deal and he is so tired.'

In her short speech she had summed up her life, her marriage, her circumstances: young, beautiful, married to a big dealer who did not like to be kept waiting.

'May I get you something, tea or coffee? Or perhaps you would like a glass of wine? We have some very beautiful wine from the vineyard of a friend of my husband.' She paused. 'A friend of ours. Would you like to try some?'

'That sounds nice, thank you.'

She rang a bell and the maid reappeared. Alessandra asked her for wine and then slipped into Portuguese.

'You speak Portuguese?' I asked after the maid had gone.

'Yes, a little,' she said.

'And I heard you speaking what sounded like Arabic to your bodyguard.'

She laughed.

'Mahmoud is the eyes and ears of my husband. He comes with me everywhere.' She said it without malice, though her tone was flat, resigned.

'What other languages do you speak?' I asked.

'Italian, obviously, English, French, Spanish and a little Russian.'

'Are you fluent in them all?'

'Oh no, my Russian, Portuguese and Arabic are very weak. I am sure Lucia does not understand me most of the time. I think she humours me.'

It was not Lucia who returned with the wine, but Mahmoud. He put down the tray and poured a small amount into each glass, less into the one he gave to Alessandra than the one he passed to me.

'My husband does not like me to drink when I am alone,' she explained, slowly turning the stem of the glass in her hand before taking a sip. 'But I am not alone.'

She turned to Mahmoud and thanked him for bringing the wine in a way that gave him no option but to leave the room. He backed out slowly, watching me, looking from the place where I stood to the low table where I had put my glass, reluctant to leave his charge with a stranger.

'I'm sorry, he is a little over-protective when my husband is not here.'

'What does he think I am, a dyke or a pusher?'

She laughed again, more relaxed.

'It is his way, pay no attention.' She finished her small glass and poured herself another one. 'The shawl you have, is it for sale?' She took a long sip from her glass, still holding the bottle in her other hand.

'Well, I suppose so, but I think there is a misunderstanding. I think you're under the impression that it's a *shatoosh*.'

'It's not?'

'No, it's one hundred per cent pashmina, embroidered in silk, four months' worth of embroidery. Would you like to see it properly?'

'Of course.'

I opened my bag and unearthed the roll of tissue paper, pausing for a moment before undoing it in front of her. The shawl rippled open across my lap. Even in the short time since bundling it into my bag, I had forgotten the detail of its beauty, its delicacy. I did what Manzoor had done, I let it fly, filling it with air and allowing it to settle on Alessandra's knee. She lifted it between her hands and buried her face in it.

'Are you sure that it isn't *shatoosh*?' she asked again.

'Yes, I'm absolutely sure.'

'And the embroidery took four months?'

'Yes, four months.'

'And how much is it?' She picked up her glass again.

'Seven hundred pounds.'

It sounded so much to me. I knew it would mean nothing to Alessandra, but I still wanted to justify the price. I told her about DRAG and the slum schools. There was silence at the end of my speech.

She drained her glass.

'This man you say who started it, he gave up everything?' she asked.

'No, he didn't give up everything, but he gave up his media career and the standard of living that went with it.'

'And he was very successful in his career?'

'Yes, he was.'

'Is he happy now?' She leant towards me.

'I don't really know. I think sometimes, when he is with the children, he is incredibly happy, but there are times when it is terribly hard, when he is fighting for funding or the government throws up obstacles. I think he despairs of the human condition.'

'My husband does not wish to have more children. He has some from a previous marriage and his relationship with them is not so good.' She went back to the table and poured herself another glass but she stopped when it was half-full. 'I am so sorry, how rude, would you like some more?'

'No, thank you.'

'I would like very much to buy the shawl. Do you take credit cards?'

'No, I'm sorry, I don't.'

'I will have to wait then until my husband comes back from the States. Then I will be able to pay you in cash.'

We agreed that she would call me and I would come over again when she had the money.

'Do you have some pictures of the children from the schools?' she asked.

'Yes, I do.'

'Will you bring some of them with you, please?'

'Of course, it would be a pleasure.'

CHAPTER 7

Money in
the Sock Drawer

MANZOOR RANG AT seven-thirty the next morning. He wanted his money.

'You can pay me cash?' he demanded. 'You can pay me today?'

'No, Manzoor, I thought I explained yesterday. I won't be able to clear it through the bank that quickly.'

'So when are you paying me?'

'I am seeing my partner on Thursday. He'll give me the money then.'

'This is very good. So you will give me money on what day?' he asked.

'I can give it to you on Friday.'

'Then I am calling to you on Thursday to make arrangements.' There was a note of panic in his voice. This was not the tone that he had used to tell his cousins, uncles and me stories on the cushions in Southall.

'My partner will not agree to give the money to me until I can give him a guaranteed delivery date for the late stock. Christmas is only two weeks away now and we need to get more shawls.' I felt it was early enough in the morning to be ruthless.

Manzoor was silent at the other end of the telephone.

'Did you hear me?'

'We will be discussing this thing when I am seeing you with the money,' he insisted.

'Will you still be staying at the Sheraton?' I sounded waspish.

'No, this place is too much of money. I am at Southall now. It is the place that you were coming to. You are knowing this place of my cousins.'

'I'm afraid I am not going to have time to come out to Southall again. Everyone in England and especially in Southall is trying to do their Christmas shopping. You must have noticed how bad the traffic is. Aren't you going to be coming into central London at some point?' I asked.

'This is too hard for me. Travelling around places in your city is too much for me. So much of peoples everywhere and no one is helping. You are understanding this problem.' Manzoor sighed.

'I will only be able to pay you if you can get into central London.'

'Is it possible that you are sending money to me?'

'You must be joking! It simply isn't safe to send that amount of cash.'

'So perhaps we are meeting nearby to Sheraton?' Manzoor had capitulated. The Sheraton Park Towers had become the triangulation point in his mental map of central London.

'Yes, I'm sure we can work out something around there.'

The meeting-point was not important. What mattered to me was that Manzoor had agreed to my terms for the first time. He wanted the cash.

Robin was less enthusiastic about handing over so much of our worth for unseen goods.

'I'm not sure that it's a terribly good idea. I mean, do you really trust him?' He was on his way to a party, driving and talking on his mobile at the same time.

'Hillary Clinton did.'

'That proves less than nothing,' Robin shouted. He sounded as if he had his head in the glove compartment.

'Well, with four shops in Delhi, headquarters in Srinagar and customers all over the world, including Harrods as of yesterday, I don't think he is going to disappear into the pale blue yonder with our smallish pile of cash.'

'It may be small in Hillary Clinton terms but it represents about fifty per cent of our current worth.'

'Robin, we save money if we pay him in cash in England. I'd have to pay him anyhow as soon as I arrive in Delhi next week. If we do it this way we avoid having to pay commission on travellers' cheque transactions at both ends,' I explained.

'Can't hear you, you're breaking up,' Robin yelled.

I could hear him as he swore at his phone, at me and at the world in general. I put down the receiver.

Thursday, the day I was supposed to meet Robin for the cash hand-over before rolling it straight on to Manzoor was another day packed with the workings of Goat. I had a meeting with a very private design house that had heard about our pashmina through the fashion grapevine. The atelier was right in the heart of Fulham, in a small yard just off the main road to the river.

Fulham ended as I rang the bell. A Frenchwoman answered and buzzed me into a world of scented candles and exotic flowers in chiffon-wrapped vases. She led me along a corridor lined with black-and-white fashion shots and into the showroom. It was a light, white room, a deep sofa at one end and a low table in front with a hat here, a rope of rough pearls there. The house collection hung around the edge of the room in fluid fabrics, perfect pieces exquisitely made, each one crying out to be touched and caressed.

I was left alone with the empty clothes. An oyster chiffon dress fluttered in the air of the closing door. I was in my street uniform, drawstring waist, baggy knees, shapeless behind, sagging neckline. I caught my reflection in the great picture mirror at the end of the room, a poor imitation of a saleswoman and purveyor of luxurious shawls. I tried tightening the drawstring and rearranging my sagging neckline but to little effect.

A porcelain blonde came into the room, tiny, delicate and sculpted into black, not a corner of material to spare, not a seam out of place. Her smile was as wide as her face was small, and her soft voice matched the summer sky of her eyes. Behind her came another blonde, long and lanky, her arms held wide, her head thrown back, the smell of a recently smoked cigarette on her skin.

'Hi, fantastic of you to come.' The lanky blonde crossed the room at a run and dived into the pile of shawls that I had stacked up on the sofa.

She managed to untie raffia, unwrap tissue paper, talk, laugh and move around the room at the same time. The porcelain blonde sat in neat order on the edge of the low table, running her hands over each of the shawls as they exploded from her partner's hands.

'Just completely gorgeous. How about if we give you our spring collection colours to match? Would that work?' The lanky blonde waved at their collection on the rails, from oyster chiffon through nutmeg, amethyst, dove and silvered sage.

'Your clothes are very beautiful. It would be a great pleasure to match-dye for you.' It seemed so easy.

'Thank you,' said the porcelain blonde quietly.

'I would love to be able to wear your clothes.' I sounded weak.

'Why shouldn't you?' the porcelain blonde asked.

'I mean I would love to be able to afford your clothes.' I was not sure if that was really what I meant, even as I said it.

'Oh, but you get to tie yourself up in all that fabulous pashmina,' the lanky blonde cried from the mirror, as she wrapped herself in pale turquoise and tea-rose.

'Yes, I suppose I do.'

The blondes had said all they could to make me feel comfortable, and yet I felt totally inadequate and formless in the face of so many hand-finished seams and bias cuts.

'If you ever want anything made, please let us know and I promise we'll give you a fantastic price,' the lanky blonde offered.

The porcelain blonde nodded her head in agreement and left the room to collect the cuttings from which I could match the dyes. She returned with a piece of stiff ivory card, the different colours pinned like tiny flags to it, labelled and coded.

'I've been seeing some really exquisite embroidered shawls around. Can you get any of those?' she asked.

'I can, but the best place to get them is directly from the weavers in Kashmir.'

'Are you going back to Kashmir soon?'

'I'm trying to,' I replied.

'Is it safe?' she asked.

'There are safer places.'

'So that means it's not very safe at all?'

'I'll tell you when I come back with beautiful Kashmiri embroidered shawls for you,' I said.

'Please be careful. You don't want to become a fashion victim of the wrong kind.' She smiled gently.

The Frenchwoman who had let me in led me back down the corridor, past the icy black-and-white images. A door to one of the workrooms stood ajar. Through it I could see chaos in motion. Computers hummed, material flew across cutting-tables and ironing-boards, women scuttled among calico-curved dummies, their mouths prickling with pins. The Frenchwoman waved goodbye to me from her chiffon-wrapped world and I headed back out into Fulham where the traffic wardens were on the march among the school-run, double-parked mothers of SW6.

At my club Robin arrived looking agitated, notepad in hand, a drooping yellow carnation in his buttonhole, not a plastic bag in sight. As he sat down he ordered something, pulled his address book from his briefcase and punched a number into his mobile telephone all at the same time. The waiter taking the order looked at me with a pained expression.

'Robin, I'm afraid you can't use that in here.'

He put the phone to his ear, waving his hand for silence. Another couple in the club, sheltering behind *The Times* and *Hello* magazine, put down their reading and frowned at me. I took Robin's telephone from him and stalked out into the corridor.

'Hey,' Robin shouted, trotting after me.

Once in the hall I gave the telephone back to him.

'You clever girl, reception's much better out here.' He resumed his loud conversation without missing a beat.

I retreated back inside. The waiter returned with Robin's order, tea and lots of biscuits.

Two minutes later Robin was back. 'Bloody things don't work at all, couldn't hear a thing that she was saying. Sometimes I can't see the point of them. They just annoy me.' He perched on the sofa next to where I had spread myself.

'Pour me some tea.'

'Pour your own tea,' I snapped. I was writing out the details of my visit to the design house, pen in one hand, notes in the other.

'You're not in a very good mood today,' he said, splashing tea.

'My mood is fine but you are not allowed to use mobile telephones in the club and I am writing, so it's hard to pour tea as well.'

'I see.' Robin broke a biscuit in half, scattering crumbs across his front, the sofa and the floor. 'Now, cream-coloured shawls – when could you send them?'

'Until I get back to Delhi and see the reserved stock that we are paying for now I'm not actually sure whether it exists or what exactly we've got.'

Robin stopped chewing. He went white and then flushed.

'Oh shit!'

'What's the matter?' I asked.

'I've only gone and forgotten the bloody money.' His flush deepened.

'Where is it?' I asked.

'Does it matter? The point is, it's not bloody well here.'

'Is it in London or Nottinghamshire?'

'It's in my sodding sock drawer, isn't it?' He stuck his face into mine.

'Not exactly my fault, Robin.'

'Oh fuck it!' He looked shrivelled.

'It's not a problem,' I said.

Robin paused. 'You're absolutely right, it's not a problem at all. I can give it to you on Monday when we have our pre-Christmas dinner. What a relief!' He unknotted his fingers.

'I'm afraid it's not quite that simple. I'm meeting Manzoor tomorrow to pay him before he goes back to India on Saturday.'

Robin crossed his arms tight across his chest and closed his eyes in pain.

'How about if you ring the bank now and tell them that I will be going into my local branch tomorrow to collect the money? Then you can retrieve the pile from your sock drawer and put it back in the bank.' I sounded just like a kindergarten teacher.

Robin jumped up. 'Right, have you got a phone? My battery's fading. I'll call them right now.'

'No,' I lied. My mobile was in reception, where obedient club members left them. 'They have a public line at the desk that you can use.'

'Okay, I'll call our manager and talk to him. Then you can fax him to confirm what time you'll be collecting the money.'

'No, I'd rather you sorted it out,' I said. Robin was a master of delegation but this time I was not going to be delegated to.

'What do you mean, no?' He was almost dancing on the spot.

'I mean I am re-delegating to you the responsibility for resolving your own mistake. I was going to call you this morning to remind you but I thought you might think I was being patronizing.' I paused. 'Sorry, that was cheap.'

'Patronize me? I would have been delighted. Why on earth didn't you, you silly girl?'

'I'm sorry.' I did not feel or sound terribly sorry.

Robin looked hurt and confused.

'It's fine,' I said, beginning to feel guilty. 'We'll work something out. But if I can't give Manzoor cash tomorrow I think it is unlikely that we'll get this reserved stock.'

'Oh dear.' Robin shrank into the sofa.

We hurried through the practicalities of sorting out the situation. The bank was called, oil was poured, and the waves became ripples. We covered the rest of our agenda succinctly and with as much grace as we could both muster, then moved on to ask about each other's families. Everyone was well, as everyone always is when you are trying to end a meeting.

Peace had been restored.

'Please, don't forget to chase up the money at the bank,' I said as I kissed him goodbye.

'Salt in my wounds.' He smiled.

'And please, please can you try not to do something like this when I'm in India trying to pay weavers directly up in Kashmir?'

'I wouldn't dare.' He waved as he bumped his way through the crush of Christmas shoppers on the King's Road.

The next day, I found Manzoor standing in the hall of the Sheraton, again small and contained within the folds of his *feron*.

Beside him stood a young boy, even smaller and neater. He too wore a *feron*, but instead of the usual white embroidered *topi*, his was embroidered in bright colours, more of a hat than a cap. Over the top of his *feron* he wore an anorak with an expensive logo. Manzoor had a small rucksack on his back.

I shook his hand and the boy's as well. He smiled from behind huge brown eyes, his nose wrinkled with embarrassment.

'This is my son.' Manzoor put his hand on the boy's shoulder. It was Ahsan, his youngest son, whom I had met in Delhi at the shop.

'Is Ahsan at school here as well now?' I asked.

'No, no, he is at very finest school in Srinagar,' Manzoor said with pride. 'He was coming with me to take other childrens back to school. I was hoping, *inshallah*, to find place for him at Manchester school now, but he does not have enough of years yet. He will be going to this school when he has twelve years. He will be joining his brothers and making me so much of a proud father.' Manzoor lifted his eyes to the heavens.

'How old are you, Ahsan?' I asked.

'I have ten years.' He stood up straight as if to seem older.

We sat in the same tea-room as before, Manzoor opposite me and Ahsan between us. Opening my day-book, I lined it up with my invoice book and my order forms. Manzoor looked ill at ease, his eyes flicking from me to the other people moving around him. He clutched his backpack in his lap. I borrowed his calculator to work out the rupee conversion rate on the money that I owed him. It took some time. Each key on the calculator had four or five different functions.

Manzoor kept reaching out to take the calculator from me and then withdrawing his hand. I could see him looking at my bag on the floor. It was the only place his money could be. We established exactly what he was owed and then I took out the money. It was in a large brown envelope, stuffed to its limit. I held it out to him.

'Would you like to go somewhere to check it?' I asked.

'No, no, this is more than fine.' He bundled the envelope quickly into his pack, zipped it up and wrapped both his arms around it.

'Would you like something to drink, tea or coffee? Ahsan, would you like something?' I asked.

'No, no, I am well and Ahsan has his thing.' Manzoor pointed to a plastic bottle of fizzy drink that his son was holding. It was the colour of a motorway cone, much too orange for safety. Manzoor held out his hand to stop me from trying to offer them anything more.

'Your Oxford Circus, how am I getting to this place? He is wanting to go there.' He put his hand on Ahsan's shoulder again.

'It's just a few stops away by Underground but it's not a great idea to go now. The rush-hour is about to start and you would be hitting the worst of the Christmas shoppers, people rushing in on their way back from work, everyone in a bad mood, everyone pushing and shoving.'

Manzoor held his head in his hands. 'In this place all the time is rushing. It is hurting my head.'

'And you think it is any better in Delhi?' I asked.

'Of course is as bad but in Delhi many peoples are doing things for you so it is not seeming so hard. Here I am having to be doing everything for myself, travelling tuck, tuck with many peoples.' He slapped his hands together and clicked his tongue at the horrors of London's public transport. Manzoor never had to use Delhi's battery-chicken public bus service.

A waiter was hovering beside us.

'I think we have finished, thank you,' I said.

He looked surprised. There was nothing on our table except my books and papers and Ahsan's alarmingly orange fizzy drink.

Manzoor stood up and waved his son to his feet.

'Do you have to go to Oxford Circus?' I asked as we made for the door.

'I have to buy *kerket* bat for very good friend of mine,' Manzoor explained.

'But you have the best cricket bats in Kashmir. What about Mr Hakim, the king of cricket-bat makers, on the Anantnag Road?'

'Of course, this is very true, we are making best *kerket* bats in the world from willow of Kashmir, but I am making promise to my friend. He is asking me for, ah, what is it?' Manzoor unzipped his pack and pulled out a small green notebook. 'See here, I am writing this thing. Now this is name: Surridge. This is *kerket* bat he is wanting.'

'Of course. But why Oxford Circus?'

'I am being told by peoples that this is best place for going to find greatest of *kerket* bats.'

I had just started to explain that a visit to Lillywhites might be more sensible when Manzoor stopped on the pavement. A Eurasian girl in platform trainers and leather jeans was trying to walk round us. She stared at the slight Kashmiri in amazement. He stared back at her shoes. The platforms at the front were probably about four inches high and those at the heel were verging on the absurd. Manzoor continued to stare as she made her way down the street through the crowd. Then she turned around and stuck her tongue out at him. There was the flash of a silver stud. Manzoor recoiled in horror.

'Oh my God, this is a most terrible thing that has been done to this poor girl! Most awful violation of woman! Who is doing this thing to her?' he asked, shaking his head and holding tightly on to Ahsan's hand.

'I don't think anyone did it to her. She probably did it herself.'

'You are telling me that she was making this thing by her own hand, in her mouth?' His face twisted in pain.

'No, she would have paid someone else to do it for her.'

'You are telling me that she was paying *money* to have this thing done?' His voice rose in disbelief and he put his hand to his chest as if he was finding it hard to breathe. 'What is this thing? What is happening to these young peoples? I am saying again that this is not good place.' He pulled his son closer to his side. 'What to do? So much of bad in Kashmir and so much of bad in this place at same time. What place is there that is good place for my childrens?'

'Please don't worry, Manzoor. People have been body-piercing for ever. It's just another sign of teenage rebellion.'

'And what would these peoples be doing if they were having guns put into their hands? It would be same in London as it is in Kashmir.' Manzoor was working himself up, clutching Ahsan with one hand and plucking at the collar of his *feron* with the other.

'She was probably a bored rich kid who did it to shock her parents and impress her friends. That's all. I don't think it neces-sarily means that she is going to start planning acts of terrorism. Manzoor, it's fashion. At the moment everyone is getting bits and pieces of themselves pierced, teenagers, the night-clubbing set, even middle-aged people who really ought to know better.'

'What is my stage, am I this middle-age?'

I knew Manzoor was about forty-six.

'Perhaps you might be at the lower end of middle age, though I think most men are in their prime in their forties.'

Manzoor would not be side-tracked.

'You are saying this thing to me that people my age are having this kind of torture to them?'

'A few, but please believe me, they are not a threat to society. It's a ridiculous quirk of fashion.' I smiled.

Manzoor muttered something under his breath and continued to cling to Ahsan.

'Are you going to go to the Underground station?' I asked, trying to change the subject.

'First of all to Harrods,' Manzoor announced in a calmer voice.

'I thought you had finished at Harrods.'

'Business is done but I am wishing to see my carpets displayed in number one shop in whole of world. Then after we have been seeing Wangnoo carpets in Harrods we will be taking Underground to your Lilywhish. It is a good place?'

'Lillywhites? Yes, you'll find every piece of sports equipment you could want.'

Manzoor shook my hand. 'I am waiting to be seeing you in Delhi again. I think it is better for us to be meeting there than in all of this push, push bad London.'

'I'll see you next week then, or perhaps in Kashmir.'

Manzoor's reply was noncommittal.

I waved them off down the street, picturing Manzoor standing in the carpet department of Harrods, slight and neat, his pack on his back, Ahsan's hand tightly held in his, drinking in the sight of his carpets displayed in the world's number one shop.

'Don't forget, Lillywhites is on Piccadilly Circus, not Oxford Circus,' I shouted after them as they turned the corner into Knightsbridge, but they were out of earshot, swallowed up in the crowd.

CHAPTER 8

Tea with Mr Butt

IT WAS TIME for me to return to Delhi. I had stock to look at that had now been paid for, I had articles to write about Kashmir and documentaries to research, I had my ticket and I had booked in with my landlady there. But first I needed to ask a question.

I rang my greatest friend in Delhi for an update on the Kashmir situation. The short paragraphs of concern in the broadsheet newspapers were becoming longer articles of alarm. Tension in the valley was mounting.

'What's going on?' I asked him.

'There are some problems in Kargil,' he replied calmly.

'Any more so than usual?'

'Not really.'

'Do you think it is safe to go up there?' I pressed.

'You're asking the wrong person.'

'Why?'

'Because you never listen to the advice I give you. My advice is the same as it always is – don't go to Kashmir.'

'As simple as that?

'Absolutely.'

The day before I was due to leave there was an extended news report on the recent spread of Islamic fundamentalism and particularly the Taliban movement in Afghanistan. The report focused on the Taliban's youth camps. It was believed that there was a system in place to train new recruits using experienced members of other terrorist groups, from ULFA, the main separatist group in Assam in the north-east of India, from the Taliban itself and from mujahideen cells in Kashmir and Pakistan. A correspondent reported from Kashmir. He talked about children who'd gone missing from villages in Pakistan and Kashmir. He gave his report against the backdrop of a scene of prayer at a mosque. It was the Hazrat Bal mosque, not far from Nagin Lake, Srinagar.

Omar, son of Mr Khan of Khan Taxis, drove me to Gatwick. It had snowed during the night – only half an inch, but the travel news was reporting doom across the country as the roads and railways ground to a halt.

Omar, however, was wholly confident of the road-holding ability of his eight-year-old Suzuki Swift as we skated blithely through the back streets of south-west London. He ignored the traffic warnings and slotted a Hindi film soundtrack into the dashboard cassette-player. Despite being a good Muslim from Lahore, Omar was besotted with the Hindi pantheon of film-stars and could rank his top ten of both sexes without drawing breath. It made him immensely happy that the leading three male stars were also good Muslim boys who all bore the same family name, Khan. Omar glowed at the very thought of it. He was famous by association. One of the three, Shah Rukh Khan, was also a favourite of mine. He had an educated sharpness about him when he was interviewed that was rare. Omar was delighted to hear of my preference and, as the snow-muted suburbs slid past, a long discussion ensued about the merits of Shah Rukh's most recent performance.

The film, which had broken the international box office record for a Hindi production, had been unusual. Instead of the standard plot in which boy meets girl, boy gets girl, boy loses girl and boy gets girl back, this film had the boy and the girl blowing each other up in the midst of a terrorist suicide bomb mission.

The theme of the film took me neatly on to my favourite topic.

'What do you think about Kashmir?' I asked Omar, as we headed for the slip-road on to the M25.

He slewed elegantly across the lanes before responding.

'I have no view.'

'How come? Everyone else seems to.'

'It is the same question that all my passengers ask. If they have ever been to India or Pakistan they seem to think that I will have some great opinion about this thing. Just because my family comes from Lahore it does not mean that I have to have a view about a place that I have never been to.'

'A lot of people who have never been to Kashmir have very strong opinions on the matter,' I replied.

'Not me.'

'So you really have no view?'

'No.'

He stared at the car in front of us. It was moving slowly but Omar made no attempt to overtake. He was clearly preoccupied. I steered him back on to the subject of films. He responded but his answers were short. The conversation fell away and I listened to another stirring version of the theme song from the film that we had first discussed.

We stopped at traffic lights on the road to Crawley. Omar turned to me. His forehead was drawn tight.

'It is a crime, all of it is a crime,' he announced.

'What do you mean?'

'Kashmir is part of Pakistan. It is our right.' He banged his hand on the steering-wheel.

'I'm not sure I understand what you mean by it being your right?'

'People of Kashmir are people of Pakistan.'

The traffic lights changed but we did not move.

'I thought that you did not have an opinion?'

'You pushed me to this point. Of course I have an opinion. I am a Muslim, I go to the mosque, I listen to what people are saying. It is a crime to try and make Muslim people part of a Hindu country.' Omar spoke with a passion that verged on the edge of hatred.

'But according to the opinion polls a majority of Kashmiri Muslims would rather have *Azadi* than be part of Pakistan.'

'This is not true.' Omar hit his fist against the windscreen.

We were still stationary at the traffic lights.

'The light is green.'

'Sorry.' But he made no attempt to put the car into gear.

'No, Omar, I'm sorry, I didn't mean to push you about Kashmir. I was just interested to hear your thoughts.' I was embarrassed at having provoked such a strong reaction at seven o'clock in the morning.

'What is it with you people and Kashmir? Do your friends come from India to your home and ask you about what your government is doing about the bad mess they have been making in Ireland for so long?'

'You are right. I know that my Indian friends wouldn't ask about Ireland,' I replied.

In suspended animation, somewhere over Istanbul, and confronted with a tray of uniformly brown food, I thought about Omar's response to my questions about Kashmir and of my last visit there in 1992.

Kashmir is beautiful, a fecund valley, coveted by every invader of the subcontinent. *Chinar* trees lie beneath soaring mountain peaks. Along a road swept by willows a man drives his load of walnuts, standing in his cart like a charioteer, flapping the reins at a tiny pony. In the pleasure gardens of the Moguls, couples

All is reflected in the lakes

wander amidst the flowers. And all is reflected in the lakes, the mirrors of the valley.

The new city of Srinagar is not beautiful. All the clutter of modern Indian life has tumbled in on it. In addition, it is a city frequently under siege, often under military curfew, regularly bombed and shot through. Almost every building in Srinagar is bullet-pocked. No one bothers to make repairs. It would be pointless. And in the summer months, when the belching freight lorries, unhindered by snow or monsoon, can get in and out of the valley, its narrow streets are choked with these monstrous behemoths, their drivers leaning from open cabin doors to spit long trails of deep-red *paan* out on to the streets or on to unfortunate passers-by.

The lorries drop off crates of Coca-Cola, videos and chemical dyes brought up from Delhi. On the return journey they carry carpets, papier-mâché trinket boxes, crewel-embroidered rolls of wool and shawls, valley crafts brought from the godowns of the old city where the wealthy Hindu merchants of Kashmir used to ply their trade from behind the pretty casements of their wooden homes. Now their houses have been burnt out by the militants, the Hindus have gone and the old city is quiet. Those that trade these days are Muslim, and even they are forced to take their wares to Delhi. Kashmir is no longer good for business.

On the eve of my visit in 1992 I had been told how to behave by my Delhi landlady.

'Keep your eyes down when you fly into Srinagar. Even if you look up for a moment the touts will descend. Eye contact is the first step in a sale. Keep your head down and take a taxi straight to Nagin Lake. Do not even listen to what they are saying. They are all liars. They will just be setting traps for you. One more thing most important to remember. They are desperate now money has gone down to nothing since the trouble started again.'

The 'trouble' had started in January 1990 when Islamic militants took over Srinagar city. In response the army and the

Kashmiri police were given extraordinary powers of search and arrest. A vicious circle of retaliation and revenge had begun.

Now, in 1992, the airport was almost empty. It was mid-April and for the local carpet-sellers, papier-mâché makers, jewellers, shawl merchants, cedarwood carvers and houseboat owners the season should have been climbing into overdrive. In happier years, over half a million Indian tourists, predominantly honeymoon couples, had visited the valley annually, along with about 60,000 foreign tourists. But now even backpackers, normally the most determined of travellers, had started to listen to the warnings of their respective foreign offices and embassies, and had stayed away. The traders were frightened. Business had never been as bad as this before. Still, my taxi-driver did his best to sell what Kashmir had to offer.

'I am thinking that you are wanting to see finest of houseboats. I am taking you to see most supa-delux of all on Dal Lake. You will not believe it.' He smiled.

'I would like to go to Nagin Lake please, to the jetty at the end of the apple orchard road, next to the old Chinese chemist,' I replied.

'You have been coming to Kashmir before this time?'

'Yes, I have been a few times.'

'Then you are perhaps knowing some of our beautiful places, but I can show you places that are hidden from most of the people.'

'That is very kind of you but I have friends who are going to look after me, thank you.'

'Where is your husband?' He leant over the front seat to look at me more closely.

'He is working in Delhi, he will be joining me in a few days.' I had bought a wedding ring to avoid long explanations.

'Then first few days will be finest of time for you to be making Kashmiri shopping. My brother has most important of Kashmiri emporiums. You will be loving to see his pieces. I will be taking you there.'

'Thank you, but I have not come to shop this time.'

'This is not shopping, only looking, only taking tea with me and my brother. Only to buy if you wish.' He started the taxi.

There followed fifteen miles of advice on shopping, all the way to Nagin Lake.

'I am thinking that you must join me and my family for Kashmiri feast. You are knowing this place and will be enjoying feast.'

I remained silent.

'My cousin is most respected and respectful guide. He will be taking you for trekking to Amarnath for seeing Shiva *lingam*. You will be finding this most fulfilling experience of your life. I am knowing this to be true.'

To travel to Amarnath is to make one of the most holy of Hindu pilgrimages. Each year the devout climb in their thousands through the hills to see a sacred ice stalagmite phallus representing Shiva, the Hindu god of destruction, set in the cool dark cave of Parvati, the vast nurturing womb of the universe.

'I am thinking that ordinary trek would not be enough for such a good lady. I am making sure that my respected cousin will be taking you to Amarnath like a true holy man. No bus trip, but full walk from Srinagar all the way to Phalgam. Then to most beautiful glade of Chandanwadi.' The itinerary rolled off his tongue.

I knew every step. I had been there three years before. I had climbed up to the exquisite glade of Chandanwadi, past the busy tea-stalls turning over a fine profit, up to Shesh Nag, to the glacier lake that turns the colour of newborn babies' eyes in summer. *Shesh* means lake, *nag*, a serpent, this one called Janakrani and thought to live in the lake in all his monstrous glory, preying on those who venture too close to the waters of his lair.

At Shesh Nag I had camped beside the lake, enchanted by the colour of the water and desperately in need of sleep, having been kept awake the two previous nights by a Mancunian couple intent on having the loudest camping sex on record. All through the

night by the lake, other pilgrims had come to my tent to try to persuade me to move. I had thought they were indulging in mild
sexual harassment. They thought Janakrani was going to leap at
me from the waters of the lake.

The next day I had walked on past the sign on the way up to
Mahagunis Pass – 'Just a hop and you are on top'. The trail had
been littered with the panting bodies of pilgrims more accustomed
to the pavements of Delhi than the gradients of the High
Himalayas. They had not found the sign funny or inspiring. It
was the time of Sawan, the August full moon, the height of the
Amarnath pilgrimage. About 20,000 pilgrims were beating the
same path to the great ice *lingam*, a thick snake of humanity converging on the mouth of the cave where the devoted washed
themselves in the freezing, dirtied waters of the snow-fed
Amrivati stream, some scraping *vibuti*, blessed dust, from the cave
walls to sprinkle over themselves before worshipping at the
lingam. Their determination amazed the foreigners who had
joined the pilgrimage. Fat, old, unfit, infirm, clinically mad, the
Indian pilgrims had all barged towards the cave, while the foreigners hovered on the edge of the mêlée with bemused expressions
on their faces. And all the while the perennial crowd of police had
kept the pilgrims in check with *lathis* and lung power. It had been
neither an easy nor a quiet trek.

My taxi driver finished his itinerary with a long speech extol-
ling the virtues of the Shiva *lingam*.

'But you are a Muslim. Why are you encouraging me to go on a
Hindu pilgrimage?' I asked.

He stopped the taxi and turned round to face me.

'If you are taking this pilgrimage it is going to change your life.
See, I am open man, all Kashmiri Muslims open men accepting of
all things and all peoples. I will give you best of all rates, no one
will give you rate so good.'

'I have done the Amarnath pilgrimage. It was wonderful, but it
didn't change my life.'

He was undeterred.

'Perfect, then you must most definitely be going again to try for big change on this occasion.'

We arrived at the lake just as the sales pitch reached its climax. Mr Butt, Nagin Lake houseboat owner, whom I had come to know and like on previous visits, was there to rescue me, opening the taxi door with a flourish.

'Welcome, dear madam. How fast is this year going. But most important is you are back to us.'

Mr Butt was a Kashmiri first and foremost. His belief in Islam came second. It was neither ambivalent nor strident. He was a local contradiction – a relaxed Muslim. He wore the *feron*, but his head was capless and he was clean-shaven. His body was as relaxed as his beliefs. Having rejected the disciplines of fasting and prostrations to Mecca, his profile had gone at the seams and he filled out his *feron* on all sides. His smile was enthusiastic and, unusually for a local Kashmiri, he sported a set of perfectly spaced white teeth.

Mr Butt ushered me from the taxi while the driver continued to extol the virtues of a second trip to Amarnath. Mr Butt slammed the door and told him to get going. Then he led the way to his boat, confidently leaving my luggage on the side of the road. I raised my eyebrows.

'Who would steal from guest of Mr Butt? You must be knowing the value of my good name here. What is this thing you are supposing?'

The afternoon was almost over by the time Mr Butt showed me on to the boat. As we stood on the veranda at one end, the muezzin was calling the faithful to prayer, his voice skittering across the water like a skipping pebble.

Mr Butt sunk his hands deep into the pockets of his *feron*.

'You see, I would be going to prayer but I am such a busy man. I am not having time for all of these things.' He rocked himself deep into one of the cushioned chairs on the front deck of his boat.

'*Princess Grace*, such a boat,' he sighed. 'What are we to do if we are going to prayer all of the times? If I am at this time walking to Hazrat Bal mosque, who would have been in this place for meeting my good friend come back to us after whole year of time away?'

I didn't reply. While he talked the daylight dropped away, leaving long pale coral shadows of *chinar* trees spilling into the edge of the lake. A white marsh stork looped its neck over its back before plunging through the tip of a shadow in pursuit of something beneath the surface. In the centre of town, in the old city, the narrow streets were mutilated and tense, watched over by Indian army soldiers, through gun-sights, from behind sandbags. There was constant noise in the city. On the front deck of *Princess Grace* the calm was only rippled by the muezzin's call and the splash of the stork.

'Will my friend be taking Continental or Indian meals? But how rude I am being. First it is of utmost importance that you come to see all rooms of your new home. Last time, you were on *Princess Diana*, am I right?'

He was right. The year before Mr Butt had given me the honeymoon room on *Princess Diana*. Now he showed me the way inside *Princess Grace*. Her sitting-room fed into a dining-room, into a bedroom, a bathroom, another bedroom, one more and out on to a private deck at the back, each room a strange marriage between high Victorian plush and modern kitsch. Sometimes the effect was enchanting, sometimes bizarre, occasionally a faithful tribute to bad taste – on the mantelpiece in the sitting-room, between a fine crystal vase and a papier-mâché box painted with a hunting scene, stood a Barbie doll dressed in a kilt and a frilly white shirt, her hair a little balding on one side. From the middle of the boat a staircase led up to a flat roof, stretching the length of the boat and surrounded by a low carved barrier to screen semi-naked sunbathers from the passing water salesmen below.

Mr Butt was delighted that I wished to eat Indian, and more importantly, Kashmiri food. A place was laid at one end of the table in the dining-room. Supper came through from the family *dunga*, the darker, simpler boat with a kitchen chimney that smoked all day at the back of *Princess Grace*. With the supper came Mr Butt. He ordered his houseboy about, directing the dishes until they were fanned around me, and then settled himself in an armchair in direct view of my plate and watched closely as I went through the choices. He got to his feet as I finished serving myself.

'Good lady, this is not enough food. No, no, this is not good at all. My wife and daughters have been cooking all day. This food is our food, the food that my family is eating. You must have more.' He leant over me, taking the lids off the dishes again. 'Come, some more.'

A pattern was set. Each evening when I came back from my days spent around the city and out in the villages researching stories, Mr Butt sent Kashmiri *kawa* tea up to me on the roof of the boat where I always went to watch the sun go down. As supper arrived, he appeared and settled himself beside me. He refused to relax until my plate had been heaped to his satisfaction. To cope with this nightly onslaught of food I starved myself all day and even took up jogging, up and down the path along the foreshore. Mr Butt was horrified.

'What is this running?' he asked the first time he caught me, red-faced and sweating, on my return to the boat.

'I am trying to run off all your wonderful food,' I replied.

'So much of waste, what is the good of all this cooking if you are making yourself decrease with this running? It is greatest thing for me if water-taxi, that is *shikara*, is lower in the water when you are leaving than when you are coming.' And so great was his concern that he took to patrolling in the early morning to try and dissuade me from my attempts to run off Kashmiri chicken and fried lotus root.

During my first stay with Mr Butt the year before, in 1991, he had been a genuinely busy man. Despite the tension in Kashmir there had still been tourists about, and there had been other guests staying on Mr Butt's boats. A year on I had Mr Butt all to myself, and as we talked I learned more of what was happening in Kashmir.

'You know, this is a bad time for we Kashmiris.'

I nodded over my second or even third helping of Kashmiri chicken with cashew nuts.

'My daughter is to be married. How will I find for her marriage? We have no business. I am now told your Foreign Office peoples and travel peoples are telling to tourist that this is most dangerous place to come and they will die if they are coming to Kashmir. Is this so?'

'I am afraid it is,' I mumbled between mouthfuls. I tried to explain that the Foreign Office had a responsibility towards tourists, that if anything happened to them the Foreign Office would have to step in.

'But can they not see that if they are stopping tourists from coming, they are starving us?'

With a heaped forkful to my lips I paused. Mr Butt had put his plump chin pensively in his hands.

'But no danger can come to tourists. This last year three hundred children of Kashmir have disappeared. Not one man has idea where they are going. Mothers of Kashmir are weeping and no one takes even small notice. But no tourist, not one tourist, has been touched. Is this not true?'

At the time it was true. The year before, in 1991, three hundred children had disappeared and had never been traced, but no tourists had come to any harm.

Front verandas of the houseboats of Nagin Lake

On earlier visits, I had had other people to talk to, the distraction of fellow-visitors. Now I spent days and nights in solitude, my nights among the empty rooms of the *Princess Grace*, my days crossing the still waters of Nagin Lake and cycling among the quiet villages beyond the city on a bicycle that Mr Butt had proudly produced, seemingly from within the folds of his generous *feron*. I began to long for the company of women, for their banter, for the details of their daily rituals to dilute the silence that I lived within. But if I had told Mr Butt that I just wanted to sit with his wife and daughters, to be among their sounds, he would have been bemused, even hurt. Why would I want to spend time sitting with his womenfolk for no other reason than companionship?

One afternoon Mr Butt went into town. I had paid two weeks' rent in advance and had handed over the money that morning. With his newly plump bank book Mr Butt had places to go and people to see. He would be away for some time.

Mr Butt and his family lived on the *dunga* next door. His wife and two daughters knew me. I had joined them for Id-ul-Fitre, the end of Ramadan's month of fasting, during my previous stay, and I had shared *shikaras* with them as I joined them on shopping trips to the city. But on those occasions Mr Butt had been present and his wife and two daughters had been quiet.

Now Mrs Butt waved me in as I stood at the door of the *dunga*, unsure whether to enter without being invited. As she got up, pushing her hands into the small of her back, I could see that she had been filled out by the years of eating good food from her own kitchen. She was wearing a *salwar kameez*, drawstring under-trousers and a long over-garment of thick blanket wool designed to keep out the cold, a shapeless sack of a garment that dropped down from the generous shelf of her bosom. Under a purple-flowered headscarf, her hair had been gathered back in a long plait. There was an air of permanence about her, as if she had always been beside the blackened cooking stove in the Butt family *dunga*. She seemed so established, so substantial, so middle-aged, but in truth she was only in her early thirties.

Her elder daughter, Lila, was a very pretty sixteen-year-old. Nicknamed Moon Child because her skin was so fair, she fulfilled all the Kashmiri requirements for beauty – light brown hair, pale skin and smoky blue eyes. Her only failing in their eyes was that she was so thin, despite a rapacious appetite.

Aban, her younger sister, was not a pretty girl. She had inherited her father's full face and brown eyes, and had the usual valley colouring. It was made quite clear, in the way that she was treated, that Aban was considered the worker, the pack animal, while Lila was the prize, though there was a sweetness about Aban that Lila seemed to lack. It was Aban who was sent off to town to stand in the food queues with the houseboy. It was Aban and her mother whom I had seen days before, standing in the cold water of the lake, their trousers rolled up only as far as their knees for modesty, though they had stood in the water up to their thighs. Their *kameez* tunics had floated around them, puffed out like pigeon chests, the air trapped between the water and their warm bodies. They had been scraping scum off the tarred sides of the houseboat, their bare hands dipping in and out of the cold water. Lila had not been on scum-scraping duty.

For all her supposed ordinariness, I thought Aban's eyes perhaps the most beautiful that I had ever seen. As I entered the *dunga* she looked up, and the light from the entrance behind me seemed to shine back from her eyes as if they were lit from inside. Mr Butt had once joked to me that when he found a match for Lila he would have to send Aban along too, as an *ayah*, a maid. I hoped a man would one day see the beauty in Aban's eyes and be enchanted by them as I had been, before the natural sweetness of her nature was eroded by disappointment.

Mrs Butt waved Aban further into the dark interior of the *dunga* to make room for me by the door and the light. The air in the boat was heavy with the smell of cooking. Then Lila broke the silence.

'We are happy for you to be here with us.'

Mrs Butt and Aban smiled.

I asked Lila to explain what they were cooking and how they prepared it. She took me deftly through the ingredients and methods. Kashmiris are meat-eaters, as are most mountain people, and they regard the cooking of meat as a sacred thing. Mr Butt had chastised me for many days after I had once turned down the ritually offered *gayka gosht karai*, beef seared at a high temperature and then bubbled in its own juices in a pan with onions and vegetables, a method now described in Bradford, Birmingham, Southall and Sydney as Balti cooking. My refusal was a clear sign that I had spent too much time with the Hindu-*wallahs* in Delhi, the cow-worshippers as he called them.

In the dim light of the *dunga* Lila held up a small bowl for me to see.

'Our father is saying to me that you are to be taking your leave of our place,' she said.

'Yes, I am leaving the day after tomorrow.'

'This is not day after?' she queried.

For a moment I thought.

'No, it is not the day following today. One more day after that,' I tried to explain. It is hard to distinguish the days when translating from a language that uses the same word for yesterday and tomorrow, the same word for the day after tomorrow and the day before yesterday.

'This is good,' she smiled. 'Day after is anniversary day of Lila. For this day we are making special dish. You have to come tasting this dish. For Lila I am asking this thing.'

The way she spoke of herself in the third person was so enchanting that I agreed.

'We are making *Kabuli pulāv*, Afghan rice cooked slowly with fat Meymanehi raisins and Kabuli dates, and *Kashmiri kapureh*.'

She smiled and again pushed forward the small bowl that she had been holding up to my face. In it were lamb's testicles.

Lila and Aban giggled. Mrs Butt's expression remained unchanged. She had understood that Lila was playing with me even though she did not seem to speak English. She held out another dish to me.

'*Kajur*,' she prompted.

It was a bowl of dates, a luxury so far from the autumn date harvest. I took one. Lila plunged her hand in as well and then spoke again through a mouthful of dates.

'Now not so much of *kajur* for best flavouring of my *pulāv*. Pitājī, my father, will not be so happy for this. Come, we all make *pakoras* and then *dudh chai*.'

Dudh chai, milky tea, a fudge-like brew of a few tea leaves, a lot of sweetened milk powder and even more sugar: Lila had a sweet tooth.

As we settled down to cook together Aban was appointed scrubber and chopper of vegetables for the *pakoras*. I was allowed to mix together the flour and spices for the batter, though only after Lila had thoroughly checked the palms and backs of my hands to see that no dirt lurked on my pale *farangi* skin. The houseboy was ordered to make *dudh chai*, brewed up on a small kerosene stove at the back of the boat. He was not allowed in the kitchen itself but received his orders from behind the edge of a thick curtain that screened off the end of the room.

Lila watched me closely as I added *garam masala*, a hot spice mix, to the flour. She stayed my hand as I was about to sprinkle in the cumin.

'No, too much of this. Come, see.'

She took the spice from my hand and deftly split the amount in two, tossing the unused cumin out through the curtain where the *chai* was being brewed. Mrs Butt sighed. Lila ignored her and whipped her fingers through the flour, flicking a large spoonful of *ghee* from a tin into the mix, flaking it through her hands, stroking her palms with the mixture. Then she nodded to her mother who splashed in water until Lila's fingers had worked it to a smooth paste. At the end of the performance, she pushed a stray hair away from her face with the batter-free back of her wrist, leaving a smudge of flour on her cheek. Mrs Butt and Aban noticed it at the same time and laughed. Lila tried to brush it away but only added a streak of batter. Aban dropped her head to laugh and Mrs Butt stuck the back of her hand into her mouth and rocked silently. For a moment Lila teetered on the edge of dignity, her jaw set. Then she too burst into laughter.

'Mr Butt told me about all the children that have disappeared. Do you hear anything about them?'

Lila's laugh stopped abruptly. I had broken a small moment of happiness.

'What is this?' She looked at me, leaning across to get closer.

'Your father told me that hundreds of children go missing every year and nothing is really heard or done about it. I have asked in some of the villages.'

Lila shrugged.

'I have heard that the mujahideen are sending agents in, through Pakistan-occupied Kashmir and Afghanistan, to take children away to training camps in the Pamirs and Karakorams.'

Lila waved her hand to slow me down. I started again, putting it in simpler terms.

'Camps, what is this camps?' She took my arm, her fingers digging into me.

'You must have heard people talking about this,' I said.

'What is camps?' she repeated.

'Some of the people I have spoken to say that their information comes from special agents from the Border Security Force of the Indian army, who are trying to frighten them into giving information. The agents have told them about these camps in the mountains where children are being trained as part of terrorist units that can then be sent back into the valley to gather infor-

mation, to fight, to smuggle arms and whatever else the mujahideen are after.'

As I talked, carried away by indignation, Lila pulled me up and
out through the curtain to the back of the boat.

'Not to speak,' she said, and then she pushed me back into the
dunga and lifted a pan from a row that hung along the side of
the boat. 'For making *pakoras*.'

I did not ask any more questions. Lila talked me through what
she was doing. Aban flipped pieces of chopped potato and cauli-
flower into the batter that Lila had made and then dropped the
mixture into the pan of oil as it started to smoke on the stove. Mrs
Butt remained where she was, cleaning vegetables and testicles.
As the smell of the spices caught on the bottom of the pan and
filled the *dunga* the houseboy put his head around the curtain and
waved a battered aluminium kettle in Aban's direction. She took
it from him and scooped up a couple of *pakoras* from the pan, dropping them quickly into his palm before they burnt her hand. He
blew on them, throwing them from palm to palm. Aban did not
thank him for the *chai* and he did not acknowledge the *pakoras*. It
was just an exchange.

Next, Aban poured out four cups of tea as Lila plucked the rest
of the *pakoras* from the pan, pincering them between her long
nails and piling them on to a plate beside her. Then we sat in
silence as we ate.

I left the *dunga* as soon as I had finished, thanking them all for
their hospitality. Aban smiled but Mrs Butt's face remained fixed,
her eyes still. I had offended her. As I walked past her to leave she
got up.

'It is our greatest pleasure,' she said.

I had not realized that she spoke any English.

Lila followed me across the narrow plank that connected the
dunga to the *Princess Grace*. Then she pointed to the roof of the
boat and climbed up behind me, ducking down by the side rail.
She looked towards the city.

'Pitājī is not yet coming. Time to speak. *Mauserā bhāi* is one of childrens taken from us. Very good boy. Mātājī, my mother, is all the time crying when we are speaking of this thing.' By *mauserā bhāi* she meant her maternal aunt's son.

'I am sorry, I did not realize that your mother spoke English or understood what I was saying,' I tried to explain.

'This is not so bad thing. You are not knowing of these things.' Her expression was serious.

'How long ago was your aunt's son taken?'

'He was just small boy of maybe five years at village well with my aunt. He is boy very much loved, the only son of my aunt. Men come through village very fast taking him and throwing him in back of jeep. Then gone across to border. *Inshallah*, if he is still living he is nearing his number eight anniversary.'

'Has anyone heard anything since he was taken?' I asked.

'It is believed by some peoples that he may be in one of camp places you are talking of. Mātājī is not wishing this. She is thinking that it is perhaps better if he is dead than to be made into little man who could come to kill peoples who are loving him.' Lila tugged at a strand of hair that had come loose from her plait.

'What does your aunt think?' I asked.

Lila did not understand.

'What does your mother's sister think of the idea that her son might be in one of these camps?'

'She is dead now. Small amount of time after Azad was gone, she is dead. Mātājī is saying it is from sadness.'

'Your aunt's son is called Azad?' I asked. *Azad* means free, a sad name for a lost eight-year-old boy.

'Yes.' Lila was still tugging at the stray lock of hair and now stood up to watch the road from town for her father's return. The women did not usually venture on to the houseboat, particularly when there were guests staying.

'Do you think Azad is still alive?' I asked.

Lila's fingers fell from her hair.

'We do not know, so it is not possible for us to have mourning for him. It is not possible for my marriage until time of mourning is past.'

'But your father told me that he was talking to his brother about arrangements to find a husband for you.' I had had many conversations with Mr Butt about his plans for Lila's marriage.

'Talk, talk, all is talking but nothing is happening until we are knowing about Azad,' she complained.

'Have you met any of the people that your father and uncle have been talking to?' I asked.

'People, what is this people, I will have just one husband.' She frowned.

'Do you know who he might be?'

Lila screwed up her face.

'This I am not knowing.'

'What kind of man would you like to marry?'

She stopped fidgeting and squatted down beside the rail again. When she spoke her voice was almost a whisper.

'This is not good for me to say.' She stopped and looked again towards the road from town. It was empty. 'A man for me to be best of mans is not making me to live on lake, not cooking all the time in darkness, having more of houseboys and *ayahs* to be doing works.' Lila wanted to be a lady of leisure on dry land.

'Do you know anyone who would be able to offer you this kind of life?' I asked.

Her face brightened.

'My father has friend, good friend. He has a brother who is making business in America. He is rich man.'

'Have you seen him?'

'Yes.'

'What is he like?'

She stood up again and put her hand just above the level of her own head. 'This in height. And this.' She stretched her hands wide, fat and wide, and laughed.

'How old is he, Lila?'

'Some years short of Pitājī.'

My host was in his early fifties. Lila hoped to marry a short, fat, middle-aged man because his brother was doing business in America. She just wanted to stop scrubbing vegetables on the *dunga*. It seemed quite a high price to pay.

'Do you think you would be happy with this man?' I asked.

She looked at me and then at the water below.

'Marriage is not for making happy.'

We stood in silence watching as groups of men on shore made their way to the Hazrat Bal mosque for evening prayer.

'Why doesn't your father go to the mosque?' I asked.

'I cannot speak on this matter.' Her mood had changed.

'Why doesn't he like you coming on the houseboats when there are guests staying?'

Lila did not look at me as she replied, and her hand returned to the strand of hair.

'He is saying we will take Western ideas and forget our respect for Islam.' She stopped for a moment, her hand in the air in front of her, as if to push away any further questions. 'Pitājī is believing all things of Islam. If he is not going to mosque it is not meaning that he is not good Muslim. He is man who is praying at all times. He is saying to our mother, to me and Aban, that if we are listening to Western ideas we will be bad mothers to our childrens and bad wives to our husbands.' She threaded her fingers behind her neck. It was a defiant gesture, but I could not tell whether it was directed at her father's authority or at me, the personification of the West.

'Is that what you think?' I asked.

She paused and reached out to touch the sleeve of the dress I was wearing. It was a simple summer dress, almost the colour of Lila's eyes.

'I wish to be wearing clothes like this instead of the ones I have.' She plucked at the thick bulk of her tunic. 'I am thinking it is wrong for young peoples not to be wearing beautiful clothes.'

She would have looked lovely in my dress.

'Most of other things of Islam are good. We are having respect from men and we are working in their homes.' She looked back towards Hazrat Bal. 'This is as it has been always. It cannot be any other.' She checked the road once more. 'It is time for return of my father. I am leaving now.'

'Thank you, Lila.'

'You are thanking me by being present for celebrations for my anniversary day after, for eating *kapureh*.' She laughed as she headed back down to the *dunga*.

I left Kashmir the day after eating Lila's birthday testicles. They were not as bad as I had thought they might be.

Now, as I sat on the plane to Delhi, remembering that visit to Kashmir six years earlier, I could see Lila Butt's face, pale, pretty and excited by the future. It was her father who had sold me my first pashmina shawl, the flame-coloured shawl that I in turn had sold in Notting Hill to an American woman in the pouring rain.

I had assumed then that I would return to Kashmir soon, that my stay with Mr Butt in 1992 would be just one of many trips. Mr Butt had said that foreigners were safe in Kashmir, that there was no risk to tourists. But then in July 1995 six foreign tourists were kidnapped by terrorists. One American managed to escape and he was picked up by a military helicopter. Two more of the hostages were injured during a gun battle with security forces. A few days later the Kashmiri police found the decapitated body of another of the hostages, a young Norwegian actor. The captors and their remaining captives disappeared into the mountains and Kashmir's terrorism began to hit the headlines.

When I tried to go back that year I could not find an insurance company that would give me cover. The valley was on the Foreign Office's black list.

Three years on, Christmas 1998, there was still no peace in the valley.

CHAPTER 9

The Battle
of Tiger Hill

THE TAXI-DRIVER from Indira Gandhi International Airport was less talkative than Omar, son of Mr Khan. Prepaid taxi-drivers in India seldom have much to say once you have covered the late arrival of the monsoon, the number of sons they have been blessed with and the woeful amount of money they have had to part with to settle their daughters' dowries.

Delhi was wrapped in a haze of pollution and the roads were empty save the odd drunken driver, weaving his way home as the dawn came up, oblivious to his lethal state, central reservations and wandering cows, safe in the knowledge that a thousand rupees slipped to the traffic cop would get him out of any trouble. A ho-hoing Father Christmas blinked through the fog from the side of a five-star hotel, blind in one eye where his bulbs had failed.

Manzoor was a big man again in his own surroundings, spreading himself comfortably about the shop, his team of boys fetching and carrying at the run. He sent Yaseen off to find samples that were fresh in from Kashmir. He waved a younger man off upstairs to get tea and called his youngest brother, Saboor, to answer the telephone. Manzoor's son Ahsan, who had been with him in London, was still at his side. He sat testing some of his father's mannerisms when he thought he was not being watched.

He was in the middle of an officious wave when I caught his eye. His smile disappeared into his lap as he ducked down. Manzoor ruffled the boy's hair.

'Come, sit, we take tea, there is much for discussion. Such good news I have to tell you.'

Yaseen returned from the godown. He smiled, his mouth disappearing back into his beard, gentleness in his face. Manzoor grabbed the packages from him.

'See, my dear, we have new surprises for you. It is a thing so clever that it is amazing even me, Manzoor Wangnoo.' He took a shawl from one of the bags.

It appeared to be an unremarkable donkey-brown pashmina and silk shawl, just like the majority of the shawls that I bought from Manzoor. I took it and wrapped it around myself. It felt unremarkable as well, though perhaps less feathery than the shawls I was used to.

'I'm sorry but I don't really understand why this is so exceptional. It is not even as soft as the usual pashmina and silk mix,' I said.

'Ah, but you must feel it most carefully,' Manzoor urged me.

I did, and it still felt unremarkable. I passed it back to Manzoor. He took it and waved it around the gathering with all the panache of a street magician selling dreams outside Jama Masjid, the great Delhi mosque, after Friday night prayers.

'Is it not incredible? This is not just pashmina silk,' he announced in triumph.

'What is it then?' I asked.

'It is more of mixture, little bit pashmina, little bit silk but more of angora.' He grinned.

'Then it is another kind of pashmina mix?'

'Of course, but we have angora in, so it is much less costly.' He continued to grin.

'Did I ask for cheaper shawls?'

'All the time you are asking me for cheaper shawls.'

'Yes, cheaper pashmina silk shawls. That's what people want, not something that's cheaper in the first place.'

Manzoor adopted a pose of profound solemnity. I caught his son doing the same thing, his hands in prayer in front of his chest, earnest, contrite and innocent. The boy was more convincing than the father.

I waited.

'Have we not been selling you finest quality of pashmina with silk?' Manzoor asked with a great shrug.

'Yes, it is usually very good but we have had a few problems recently. We talked about these things in London and the shawl that you showed me there was very good quality again. Am I missing something? Is there anything wrong with the big batch of stock that I have just paid for?'

'No, no, my dear, it is perfect.' He slid his index finger down the bridge of his nose.

'Then what is the problem?' I pressed.

'We have been gravely deceived.' Manzoor put his head in his hands. 'While I have been away, while my good brothers have been minding to business, they have been buying from a man who is swearing to us that he was providing to Wangnoo Brothers only the highest quality of pashmina. Have you not seen yourself how much care I give to selecting of shawls? All of the time peoples have been coming to me and begging for me to buy from their supplies. And I am refusing these peoples because of their poor quality. And what is this? I go away and my brothers are being made most serious of promises that are not true.' He stopped and sighed.

'Yes?' I tried to sound sympathetic.

Manzoor raised his hands to the sky.

'We have been cheated. The shawls of which you are making complaint, the shawls that we were made big promises for, they were not coming from Kashmir at all. This bad man was selling to my brothers pashmina with silk from Nepal, not so good

178

quality, and making me pay same prices as for Kashmiri pashmina with silk.' He slumped back, his yarn spun.

'Is that it?' I asked. It was not as bad as I'd thought.

'It is most terrible deceit,' Manzoor elaborated.

'I don't think it is so bad as long as you can be sure that all the
future stock is the same quality as you showed me in London.
What has already been sold or dispatched has gone, it's in the
past.' I smiled at Manzoor.

'My dear good lady, we are most fortunate to be doing business
with you. *Inshallah*, this thing will never be arising again.' He
bowed low and his son did the same.

I laughed and Manzoor became more expansive.

'As a mark of our regard for you we are demanding of this bad
man that he is giving us very best price now. We are insisting
that he give to you the very highest quality of pashmina with silk
for the same price that you have always been paying.' He
stopped, waiting for my appreciation.

I was not overwhelmed and it obviously showed on my face.

'And further than this, as mark of high esteem in which my
family is holding you, we are making invitation to you to come
and stay in Srinagar on one of our houseboats as guest, total
complimentary with regards and good wishes of my father, of me
and all the members of my family.'

That was very good news. I hadn't heard from Mr Butt since
shortly after my last visit in 1992 when he had written to me
requesting some vests from Selfridges Men's Department. In a
valley quivering with terrorist unrest, in the midst of winter,
I needed somewhere safe to stay.

But even as I accepted Manzoor's invitation I wondered how
wise I had been. Once I had first set foot on the deck of the
Princess Grace in 1992 I had become Mr Butt's, and his alone.
Other houseboat owners had been hustled away. He had also
controlled exactly what I bought and from whom. If I stayed
with Manzoor it would mean that I would have virtually no

chance of buying from other suppliers. I would just have to see how things turned out. In the meantime I needed reassurance that the supply of shawls would not dry up.

'Where are you getting the shawls from now? What makes you feel so confident that we will not be cheated again?' I asked.

Manzoor steepled his long fingers and peered at me over the top of them.

'The goat.'

'I know they come from goats but where after that?'

Manzoor stared at me over the tips of his fingers and took a deep breath.

'We are buying fleece straight from goats and now we are going to be weaving it ourselves. Is this not one hundred per cent guarantee? How could you doubt my word?'

'That sounds very exciting. You will be breeding goats next, Kashmir to Knightsbridge with no middleman. Will I be able to meet some of your goats when I come to stay?' I asked.

I had seen flocks of goats in the High Himalayas before. They had been scattered dots grazing in the valleys as I had trudged through ice fields, exhausted, disenchanted and numbed by the altitude. The goats had represented humanity, the promise of campfires and food after the rattle of rationed oxygen in starved lungs, struggling over silent passes, stalked by the echo of avalanches. I had a fondness for goats. Now I had a chance to get closer still. I could picture long days spent in the hills with the herders, conversations with goats amidst the wild thyme and mountain strawberries.

'My dear, we will never be raising of goats. It will not be possible for you to be meeting with goats.' Manzoor looked offended.

'I'm sorry, I did not mean that I thought you should become goat herders. Can I explain?'

He nodded.

'You see in England people now want everything to seem as

close to nature as possible. We are all obsessed with everything being organic.'

'Organic, what is this?' Manzoor interrupted.

'Organic is when products come as directly from nature as possible without the use of chemical fertilizers or additives. We love everything to seem close to its natural state. People like to get things in baskets or wrapped in brown paper tied with raffia instead of in plastic bags.' I hesitated. I was trying to explain something that was anathema to the Indian mind.

Manzoor looked increasingly confused.

'Our goats are having nothing of these additives or fertilizers.'

'I know that but people will love the idea that their shawls come direct from the goats.'

'Is not possible. There are no goats in Kashmir.' Manzoor propped his head in one hand.

'No goats in Kashmir? What do you mean, I've seen thousands of them in the hills, in the villages, everywhere.'

'These are not goats for pashmina.' Manzoor closed his eyes.

'So there are no pashmina goats in Kashmir?'

'Not one,' he said with finality.

'Where are they then?' I asked.

'In Ladakh.'

Of course. That was where I had seen them – in Little Tibet, among secret valleys high up amidst the peaks, where the grass grows emerald green by streams that tumble down from the passes.

'Then why is pashmina woven in Kashmir if the *pashm* only comes from Ladakh?' I asked.

'We have the best weavers, of course,' Manzoor replied.

'And who is buying the *pashm* from the herders in Ladakh?' I persisted.

'We have peoples who are buying there on behalf of Wangnoos.'

'How do they manage to get to the herders?' The herds were

a long way from Leh, the capital of Ladakh, perhaps a day by jeep or three or four days on foot.

'My peoples are overseeing purchase of wool. They have contacts who are going out to the herders.' He smoothed out some creases in his *feron*.

'And how are you getting the *pashm* from Leh to Srinagar at the moment?'

All freight from Leh bound for Srinagar had to pass through Kargil, and the news from Kargil was mixed. A month before, in London, I had read that insurgents from Pakistan were believed to have occupied the heights above Kargil. Now, in Delhi, there was talk of the Indian army being put on high alert. There had been curfews in Srinagar and the roadblocks on the route from Leh were increasing every day. Though no one talked about it, the traffic police and sometimes even the army often seized freight and held it, supposedly for checking. A hefty fine usually had to be paid to get the goods released.

Manzoor closed his eyes again. 'There is no problem, be assured of this.'

Manzoor's confidence had a cold edge. What enabled him to move *pashm* around with such ease at a time when everyone else was experiencing difficulties? For the first time I wondered whether there might be links with militant groups.

The room seemed suddenly small and oppressive. We sat in silence as tea was poured. My friend in Delhi had been right. Kashmir was dangerous.

I had to break the silence.

'When are you going back to Srinagar?' My voice had a crack in it.

Manzoor sat for a moment without replying, his eyes still shut. Then he opened them slowly.

'I am not so sure on this thing. We are having much of snow at the moment.' He too sounded strained. 'Will you still be coming as our guest?'

'I hope so.'

I was unnerved. The warmth of the earlier invitation seemed to have gone from his voice. Had my thoughts been so transparent? With an effort I gave him a full, broad smile.

'I am very much looking forward to coming to stay with you and your family.'

Manzoor's face opened again. He seemed genuinely delighted.

'This is very good news. It is making me very happy. You will tell all your friends how perfect it is and then they will all be coming to stay on my family's houseboats.'

'Perhaps I will be able to come and meet some of the weavers?' I asked.

'Of course, it will be my greatest pleasure. I will be taking you to see so many unbelievable things. This is if snow is permitting us these freedoms of movement.'

He stroked his son's head.

'You will be having so much of peace when you are coming to my valley. You will be truly amazed.' Manzoor's words were slow and deliberate.

I could not judge whether I had been over-sensitive in my interpretation of his comments about moving *pashm* from Leh. Though links with terrorism did not fit with my knowledge of him and his family, I needed to go back to Kashmir to see the place again for myself.

On the street in front of the airline office a man lay asleep on the pavement. A small cloud of warm breath hung above his head, holding his dreams in the downdraft of winter from the Himalayas that had spread over Delhi. He was the doorman and he was not meant to be asleep. He had a small pile of numbered plastic chips in his lap that he was supposed to dole out to anyone who came in. He was the queuing system. But he was not doling, he was sleeping. It was lunchtime.

It was too cold to stand for long on the street. But still the doorman managed to doze. I stepped over him and into the office to book my ticket to Kashmir.

A young man in a blazer ignored me as I stood in front of him. He was on the telephone, in the middle of a conversation with his 'Baby'. I watched the screen-saver on his computer fade and re-focus, a famous Bollywood star's midriff blurring and clearing exactly in his sight-line. The young man turned his chair away from me. His behaviour had been borderline up to that point but now he was being rude. I hit the return key on his computer. The midriff disappeared and a booking screen came up. He swivelled back to face me, his expression loaded with righteous indignation. Eyebrows raised, I dared him. He told 'Baby' that something had come up and put the receiver down very slowly.

'Thank you,' I said.

'Welcome,' he replied.

'I would like to book a return ticket to Srinagar, please, leaving on Saturday and coming back two weeks later.'

The young man looked at me.

'Veg or non-veg?' he asked.

'Veg, please.'

He tapped the information into his computer.

'It is not possible,' he announced.

'Okay, non-veg then.'

'No, madam, you are misunderstanding me.'

'Well, what do you mean?'

'It is not possible for you to fly to Srinagar at this time.'

'Why?'

'There is a problem.'

'Obviously.'

We glared at each other.

'What kind of problem?' I asked.

'I am not at liberty to discuss this.'

'Who is at liberty?'

'You will have to be speaking to the manager.' He examined the buttons on his blazer.

'Please may I speak to your manager?'

'This is not possible.'

'Your manager is at lunch?' I guessed.

'This is very much the case,' he confirmed.

'And when might you expect him back from lunch?'

'This is depending on how long he is taking.'

'Of course. Do you mind if I wait?' I asked.

'It is my pleasure,' he said gracelessly.

I settled myself to wait, camping on a sofa beside the door to make sure that I did not miss the arrival of the manager, strolling in after his leisurely lunch. Just as I had entrenched myself, he came back, surprising both the young man and me.

'I was hoping to fly to Srinagar. Your colleague tells me that this is not possible.'

'This is correct,' smiled the manager.

'Yes, I realize this but I was hoping you might be able to give me some explanation as to why this is the case.'

'Madam, there are problems in Kashmir right now and it is not possible to fly to Srinagar.'

'But I called a few days ago to find out about the price of flights and there seemed to be no problem then.'

'Not possible,' he repeated.

'I promise you it was possible according to the charming lady I spoke to then.'

'This may have been so but now it is a different scenario.' He started to walk away.

'And you can give me no further information other than the fact that I cannot book a ticket to Srinagar?' I pressed.

'Madam, it is Christmas time,' he said.

'I know, but the planes still fly, even on Christmas day.'

The manager waved his hand in both agreement and dismissal and then walked out of the room.

As I left I tripped over the sleeping doorman. He coughed, awoke and caught the end of my shawl.

'Madam, madam, taking ticket.' He waved one of his numbered plastic chips at me but he was too late.

Manzoor was even more opaque on the subject when I told him of my failure to book a ticket.

'There is so much of snow,' he murmured over his tea.

'But surely it snows this much every year?'

'This is most heavy winter we have been having since fifty years.'

'But that is what they say every year. Every winter is the hardest one for fifty years until the next one.'

Manzoor nodded.

'You could be coming by train?' he suggested.

'Why should the trains be running if the planes are not?'

Manzoor shrugged. It was then that I noticed his expression. His eyes did not settle but flitted around the room, never resting for more than a minute at a time. He did not look at me.

'When are you going back to Kashmir?' I asked.

'Soon, I am not sure but very soon.'

'And you think you will be able to fly back?'

'Of course.' He shouted to some of the boys who were packing up freight boxes of shawls around us.

'And you think the only problem is the snow? You don't think there is anything else?'

'Just snow, this is what I am telling you.' Manzoor looked over my shoulder.

But it wasn't just the snow. A Sikh brigadier, the regimental stripes on his turban as sharp and neat as the roll of his beard, had given a press statement. The brigadier believed that the insurgents were being specially trained in a camp right on the Line of Control. He also implied that there were other forms of military build-up by 'the enemy' in the same area. He stated that he was giving daily reports to military headquarters on the situation. The implication was that the brigadier did not feel he was getting the support that he needed, that HQ was being blasé about the threat on the snowline. In response, in another press statement, HQ implied that the brigadier was getting over-excited.

I went to see Manzoor again. It was Saturday afternoon and the five-star tourists were out shopping for pashmina and silk carpets. Manzoor and his second brother Rafiq sat solemnly like Tweedledum and Tweedledee. In front of them were laid out a thermos of tea, cups and saucers, toast and squares of processed cheese. Three assistants were busy running up and down the stairs, pulling shawls in and out of calico bundles, rolling and unrolling carpets, while the brothers slowly chewed cheese on toast and directed the floor show. Each of the customers was given a code-name: green embroidery for big-bottomed American, papier-mâché candlesticks for Japanese woman with flying ears, pashmina silk for French girl showing belly to the four winds. It was not a good time to sit down and talk about a possible invasion of Kashmir.

I retreated to the upstairs room with a plastic bag full of labels that needed to be sewn on to shawls destined for the boutiques of Notting Hill. Manzoor sent one of the boys up to help me. We sat in silence over a pile of pashmina silk stitching on tags, while down below Manzoor and Rafiq bubbled and popped through their speeches on the virtues of pashmina to their customers. In the background the accountant's adding-machine tapped and turned as purchases were made and profits mounted.

After sewing on three labels my helper got up, unrolled a small green rug and began to pray beside me, prostrating himself

Yaseen surrounded by shawls in the upstairs room

in a small corner among the calico bundles. As he finished another boy came to take his place. And so they prayed in rotation, each one squatting down beside me to help sew while they waited their turn to face Mecca.

Manzoor's head appeared at the top of the stairs as the last boy finished.

'I would like to speak to you when you have a moment.'

'What is this? Problem?' he asked.

'No, well, yes, it is a problem I suppose,' I replied.

'Come, we will talk.' He shooed the boys away and settled himself among the shawls I was packing.

'What is problem?'

'When are you going back to Srinagar?'

Again the same question.

'Soon,' he said.

'And you think it is safe to go at the moment?'

'I have been telling you, there is much of snow and Nagin

188

Lake is little bit freezing. My childrens tell me today on the phone they are walking on pieces of freezing lake. And snow is falling all the days, so beautiful. You must come and see this thing.'

'I am not sure if I am going to be able to come.'

Manzoor shrugged.

'As you wish.' He paused. 'Perhaps it will be better thing if you are coming in spring. It is most beautiful time of all.' He put his hands together as if in prayer. 'Yes, in spring my valley is most beautiful, you will not believe, you must come at this time.'

It was the end of the conversation. While accusations flew back and forth between the officers on the Line of Control and those at HQ, the rest of the world celebrated Christmas and the militants began to rally in the high passes.

I returned to London just after the New Year, my arms full of pashmina dyed beside a supposedly freezing lake where I was told it was snowing more than it had for fifty years.

Once the snow melted I planned to return to India and make my way up to Nagin Lake for the beginning of the new dyeing season. I wanted to go out to the villages and meet some of the weavers, to ask if they would embroider pashmina shawls. It was not to be.

In May 1999 conflict broke out between India and Pakistan over an insurgent invasion in the heights above Kargil. Kashmir was once again on the front pages of the world's newspapers.

Each week I spoke to my friend in Delhi to find out how the war was going from the Indian perspective. Initially there was a lot of fighting talk. Jingoism rattled down the long-distance line and the phrase *Mera Bharat Mahan* – My Great India – recurred. But as the weeks passed, and the Indian Airlines flights from Srinagar carried out only body bags from Kargil, the jingoism faded.

'How many people will have to die before we all realize that there is no solution to this, that it is a blister on the sole of our foot and we will always have to walk?' asked my friend.

On the other side of the Line of Control a friend from Lahore wrote, saying that the street toy-sellers were making their fortunes out of models of Pakistan Airforce Mirages and Indian MIGs. Children were paying a premium for them and their most popular games were reconstructed dog fights in which the Indian MIGs invariably crashed. The toy-makers of Lahore were happy for the conflict to last.

When the Kargil war started in May the pundits said it would end in a couple of weeks. By mid-June they had decided that it might last until July. By the beginning of July they were less keen to venture an opinion and would only say they thought it might last longer than they had originally been led to believe.

My friend in Delhi thought it might last until September.

'But I was planning to come back in July and go up to Kashmir then,' I whined.

'Pack your pashmina flak jacket,' he said.

I called Gautam to see what he thought. He was not interested in Kargil. He had been born in 1947, the year of Indian Independence, Partition and the first Indo-Pak war over Kashmir. He had grown up with the Kashmir situation. He was waging a war of his own. He had been trying to drill a well on land bought for DRAG's organic farm. They kept hitting rock and costs were mounting.

'And we are trying to start building the community centre in one of the slums, but we do not have the money.'

Goat was raising money but the need for more was never-ending.

'So many people made promises to DRAG this year and it has all just been smoke and mirrors,' Gautam went on.

I could hear the exhaustion in his voice.

'I'm trying to get back to Kashmir to get more shawls. I'm bringing money for you.'

'Good.' But he didn't sound very enthusiastic.

In early July the Indian army stormed Tiger Hill, a frozen wasteland above Kargil that had been seized by the Pakistani army and militants. By mid-July the war was officially over. Then stories began to spread about what had really happened and who was to blame.

The insurgents had taken the heights above Kargil in May 1999.

No, Pakistan's army had started to build bunkers there as early as September 1998.

The insurgents were militant units that had filtered in from Afghanistan.

No, it was all part of the Pakistani game plan, a well-prepared military campaign to wrest Kashmir from India. The army had taken advantage of the mildest winter on record to lay cement foundations for high-altitude bunkers within Indian-occupied Kashmir.

Manzoor's description of a snow-covered valley in the grip of the worst winter for fifty years melted away. He had his reasons – militant weavers, militant dyers, or perhaps simply a reluctance to admit that his valley had, once again, become a war zone.

Once peace broke out I started to make plans to return to India. Robin began changing his stock requirements on a daily basis as my departure loomed, and my order book began to fill up.

'I want a red one, the same colour as that dress what's-his-name's girlfriend wore to that film première, you know, her tits were coming out of it all over the papers.'

'I've got a bag of aquamarines I bought on my honeymoon in Bangkok ten years ago. I'm dying to do something with them. Could I send them to you and get them embroidered on to a shawl?'

'Mummy wants one the colour of mimosa. There's masses of it in her garden in Provence. I'll send you a photograph and then you can dye it to match.'

And my favourite: 'Could you do one for me the colour of Mrs Thatcher's dress when she went to see General Pinochet about all that fuss.'

My day-book shimmered with colour – rinsed pomegranate, pale peony, deep castor, Valhrona chocolate and the colour of the Outback sky.

While I took orders, Manzoor flew from Delhi to Srinagar to be with his family. I rang him at the house by the lake. He came to the phone in a state of high excitement.

'Hello, my dear. I have new record.'

'Hello, Manzoor. What do you mean?'

'Saboor, number four brother, has record on the telephone. Ashraf, number three brother, has record in the air. Rafiq, second to eldest brother, was having record for roadside but now I am breaking this.'

I had no idea what he was talking about.

'Lady was buying carpets from Ashraf on plane and just putting money into his hand. Now my record for roadside is happening in Delhi, on street outside five-star hotel. Arab lady is coming to me and just putting $5,000 into my hand for shawls without having seen one piece. Lady sees me carrying some pieces of pashmina and she is asking me what I am doing. I tell her about shawls and that I am selling pashmina of such high quality for very good price. So I get money in my hand from her for order and she says she will pay rest of money when I send shawls to her. I am saying to her that I will write down my numbers and addresses of all my shops and I am telling her about Hillary Clinton. But she is saying she does not need any of these things and she is trusting me. Now she is sending me ticket to Jeddah and I am to go and stay and to meet all of royalty so they can be my customers.' His smile was audible.

My own reason for phoning seemed weak by comparison.

'I was hoping finally to come back to Kashmir.'

'This is marvellous news. When are you going to come? It is so beautiful now, it is sun and sweet air, not like Delhi. My childrens, my family, we are all waiting for you to come.' There was such warmth in his voice.

'I will come as soon as I get back to Delhi and can book a flight to Srinagar.'

'Oh, you are in London,' he laughed. 'I am thinking that you were in Delhi. Flight will be no problem. Just give me date when you are thinking to come to Kashmir.'

'Well, I thought perhaps I'd come at the end of September.'

'Very good news. There is something I am asking for you to bring for me,' he said.

'Of course.'

'Pringle socks, just in black, and ear thing for cell phone.'

Manzoor had seen my earpiece when we had met in London and had decided that, as a modern man, he had to have one.

There was a brief pause in his shopping-list.

'One thing more, my dear. Saboor is having small lump on finger and he is asking if you can bring something for this.'

'Is it a wart?'

There was some shouting in the background and then Saboor came to the telephone. He described the lump in detail.

'It does sound like a wart,' I said.

Saboor shouted to Manzoor that he had a wart.

'I will bring something for it,' I said.

'Wonderful, and we will be seeing you in Kashmir.' Saboor gave the telephone back to Manzoor.

'I am thinking it will be much better if you are coming to Kashmir before end September,' Manzoor said.

'Why?'

'Because by end September the lotus flowers will all be finished. And please to remember Pringle socks, earpiece and wart cure for Saboor.'

CHAPTER 10

Serpents
in the Garden

THE KASHMIRI COCKSCOMB and purple clover had drooped in September's afternoon heat. Saboor held the small bunch out to me, wrapped in newspaper and tied up with thread. My plane had arrived at Srinagar airport over an hour late and the flowers had wilted but still he handed them to me with a flourish as a soldier stuck his rifle between us. The youngest of the four Wangnoo brothers continued to smile and bowed his head to the soldier. The rifle was lifted away and nothing more was said about it as the driver took my bags and we walked across the tarmac.

'How many years now is it since you have been in Kashmir?' Saboor asked as we drove away from the airport.

'Just over seven.'

'Oh, this is too long to be away from this place. You must have been missing it so very much. When I am going to Delhi for winter I feel so much of sadness when I know I am going to be away from Nagin for so long. There is so much of pressure, so much of noise in Delhi and so much of peace here.' He turned to me and smiled as two army lorries forced our jeep on to the verge. There were soldiers standing braced in the back, black bandannas around their heads, their fingers on the triggers of their guns. They blew loud whistles and shouted at people on the roadside and at the drivers of civilian vehicles. Saboor said nothing.

We drove in silence for a while and then he turned to me.

'See our *chinar* trees, they are so beautiful. Had you forgotten them?'

I had not forgotten. *Chinar* trees still shaded the road to Srinagar but now the road was also lined with military bunkers, sandbags against their outer walls, camouflage nets thrown over the top. Rifles prickled from the netting, levelled directly at us as we passed.

We crossed a new bridge.

'This is good, Saboor, bridges being built,' I said.

He shrugged.

'Militants were blowing up the old one. Army was building small one but only they were using it.' He pointed to a narrower bridge beside the new one. 'So we were having to build new one. Many bridges were being blown up.' He wound down the window and leant out. 'See, now is most delicious time for apples and pears. We are stopping and I am buying some for you to welcome you to Kashmir again.'

We stopped and Saboor bought big red Kashmiri apples and small sweet green pears. He watched me eat them as we made our way towards the city.

'I am not eating apples much now. They are giving me problems with wind. I am liking bananas most of all but we are not growing bananas in Kashmir, no bananas, no mangoes, no oranges, but all other fruits.'

I remembered that Mr Butt had also hankered after bananas. I asked Saboor whether he had any news of the Butt family.

'Of course, we are knowing all houseboat news on Nagin.'

'How are they?'

'I am not knowing this.' He shrugged.

We stopped at some steps among the willow trees where a *shikara* was waiting to take us out on to Nagin Lake. *Dream Girl Supa Delux – Full Spring Seats*, as her signboard announced, promised long, sensual afternoons among the lotus gardens and royal bridges.

As *Dream Girl* slipped across the lake in thick autumn afternoon sunshine, the shimmering reflection of the water danced
across the swagged material above my head. A Himalayan falcon
hung on a cushion of air, watching the silver slide of the fish below
the surface.

My last *shikara* ride had been away from Mr Butt's *Princess
Grace*. I had grown to love that houseboat's quirky plumbing, her
mosquito screens with holes the size of children's fingers, her
nightly musk of kerosene, splashed into lamps in the dark by the
houseboat bearer when the electricity failed, her sighs as her
planks shifted with every ripple of the lake. I was not prepared for
the luxury of HB *Wuzmal*, Gurkha Houseboat Group, Prop. Bros.
Wangnoo.

Wuzmal means pretty in Kashmiri and *Miss Pretty* was just a
year old. I was her first European guest, her first customer since
the Kargil war. She lay at her mooring in the middle of the
Gurkha Houseboat Group of five, broad of beam, her verandas
carved with *chinar* leaves, zinnias and lotus flowers.

'This is your home now, you are as to us a sister,' said Saboor as
Dream Girl's long, fine nose rubbed on to the bottom step of
Wuzmal.

Brother number three, Ashraf, was sitting among the cushions
on deck, his hand in his beard, his face and his dress familiar
reflections of the Wangnoo family. He jumped on to the steps of
the boat as we arrived, stretching his hand out to me.

'Now you have come home,' he smiled. 'It has taken you so very
much of time.'

In procession we looked at each of the boats, Saboor ahead,
pointing out the design details of each one, Ashraf jogging
behind, stopping me in each bedroom so that I could admire the
intricacy of the crewel-work on a bedspread or the splendour of
the matching candy pink bath, basin and loo in the adjoining
bathroom. We came back to rest on *Wuzmal*, in a bedroom at the
end of the boat.

'I am thinking perhaps this will be your room,' Saboor suggested. 'It is especially lovely room and so much of peace at the back, away from all the busy, busy of the lake.'

I smiled. The dipping of the *shikaris'* blades among the lily pads, the muezzin's call to prayer from the minaret of Hazrat Bal mosque, the skimming feet of ducks coming in to land, the thud of carpet-beaters as houseboat bearers went about their daily routine – these were sounds that bubbled up from my memory of past days on the lake.

Another face appeared out of the afternoon glow as Saboor and Ashraf finished their tour of the five-boat empire.

'This is Moqbool. He will be answering your every need while you are with us. He will be all things to you,' said Saboor.

Moqbool stood on a duckboard between two of the houseboats. On being introduced he grinned, a single tooth missing from the middle of his smile, his grey beard elegantly slashed with white, almost the same colour as his pale Persian lamb hat. His feet were bare and callused beneath his long blue brass-buttoned coat, the uniform of the Gurkha Houseboats. He was tall and fine-boned, a classic Kashmiri. He bowed low, with perfect balance on the plank, his feet splayed across the narrow board as if they were webbed.

As he was leaving Saboor turned to me.

'Take some rest and come to the house for tea with my family. They are wanting to meet you. Four will be a good time.'

By the time Saboor came to collect me I had melted on to the deck amid the cushions and carpets. He led me through a meadow at the back of the boats. The only sound was of leather on willow as several teams of boys and young men played cricket, their games overlapping with each other's. Saboor marched right through the centre of play, his hands behind his back. A batsman hit a shot that sailed just over his head.

'This is Moqbool. He will be all things to you.'

'Boundary,' Saboor called out, without breaking his stride.

A lanky young man, his voice cracking on the edge of puberty, disputed the call.

Saboor stopped and turned to face him. A small cow with seductive eyelashes ambled between the two men.

'Boundary,' agreed the young man, shrugging in deference to Saboor's seniority.

Play resumed. Saboor, the cow and I watched as the bowler hitched up his *feron* to begin his run-up.

The gate to the house by the lake had a handle shaped like a dahlia. Saboor opened it and waved me into a sea of roses, zinnias, clover and cosmos lapping beneath green-gold willow trees.

'Now you are seeing why it is hard for us to come to Delhi. Look at my home. Can you understand why all we brothers are running back here at shortest possible opportunity?' He stopped for a moment and surveyed the garden. Beyond the zinnias and the roses three storeys of white-framed windows stood stacked under a steep double roof, its pitch echoing the mountains around.

Saboor called out in Kashmiri, knocking twice on the door and waiting for a moment before opening it and gently pushing me through.

'Welcome to my home. See, this is where we are sitting with peoples. Come, sit.' He pointed to one of the bolsters against the wall. Except for a silk carpet and red-silk bolsters around the wall, the room was bare. As I crouched to sit down, a little girl with almond eyes slid into the room behind her father.

'This is Suriya, my daughter.' He pushed the girl towards me, telling her to say hello.

She ducked her head and whispered the word, trying not to laugh.

'She's beautiful,' I said.

'*Inshallah*, all our children are beautiful.'

A half-lit corridor opened into the kitchen. A face appeared around the door, a smiling moon with burnished cheeks, hair tied back in a floral scarf.

'My wife Zubeda.' Saboor introduced her.

She shook my hand in both of hers, looking straight into my eyes, hers crinkling around the edges as she smiled.

Saboor waved to a figure at the other end of the kitchen. 'This is Naseema, wife of Ashraf.'

She did not move but nodded her head without speaking.

'She is not speaking too much of English,' Zubeda said with confidence.

'She is speaking no English,' Saboor corrected. And then he pointed to the front of the kitchen that was separated from the rest of the room by a low white wall. 'We will drink tea here as we do with just family.'

I made to step into the kitchen but again Saboor took my elbow.

'First I am showing you winter sitting-room, beautiful room, you will love it.'

The winter sitting-room was exactly like the summer sitting-room, only smaller.

'But thing that is as magic is we are having stones underneath floor here and in cold weathers we are having little, little fires under, so stones are hot and room is nice and warm. Sit, we will have tea here.'

I was allowed to settle and Zubeda carried in tea, put it down and returned to the kitchen. We were not going to be having tea as a family.

Saboor sat on the opposite side of the room and played with the various children who came in and out, some his, some of them his brothers', all equal under one roof. Then came the time for prayer.

'You will sit and talk with women until we are returning. It will not be long.' He called out to the kitchen and Zubeda's face came around the door.

Her English was slow but good, and when she was in doubt we managed through a mishmash of Hindi and Kashmiri.

She was thirty though her full, polished cheeks and smooth

The willow and pitched roof of the house by the lake

skin made her look younger. She had been married to Saboor for almost nine years and they had two children. Zubeda had had a difficult pregnancy with each and both had been born by Caesarean section. Saboor wanted another child but Zubeda was unenthusiastic.

'So much of pain, so, so much of pain.' She held her generous stomach and rocked on her heels.

'Did you know Saboor before you married?' I asked her.

'First time was on day of marriage.'

'That must have been quite frightening. What if you had not liked the look of him?'

Zubeda clutched her stomach again, but this time she was laughing.

'I was liking him very much.'

'And were you happy?'

'Very much but for one thing – in first week my husband was going for work with his brothers and I was sitting here for whole of day like statue.' She drew her arms to her sides, pursed her lips, screwed up her eyes and then stiffened into immobility before collapsing into laughter.

'What if you had not liked your husband?' I persisted.

Zubeda closed her eyes.

'I am being engaged for marriage by my parents when I was fifteen years.' She paused.

'And what happened?'

'I was saying to my parents that I was not to be doing this thing. I was too much of young, not knowing enough of anything.'

'And what did your parents think?'

'So much of noise and chaos. Then after some time they are seeing that it is not such a bad thing. Then when I am marrying to my husband they are very happy.'

For all her breadth and heaviness there was something in Zubeda that reminded me of Lila Butt, a single-mindedness that some Kashmiri Muslim parents might find intolerable. Before I could probe further Saboor returned from his prayers, a boy on either side of him.

'Now meet with Omar and Aqib, sons of Rafiq and Ashraf.' He pushed the two boys forward.

They nodded, grabbed some biscuits from the plate in front of me and ran off into the garden.

We settled for more tea.

'Did Manzoor tell you about how he is making new record for family?' Saboor asked.

'Yes, he did, the new Wangnoo roadside record,' I said with enthusiasm.

'*Inshallah*, we are more than lucky in our business. In the time of our father and of his father and on for five generations we have been in the business of houseboats. I will show you some letters we have been receiving from peoples far back to times in 1800s. I must show you these things.'

'But you do not rely on the houseboat business now?' I asked.

Moqbool had had to think hard when I asked him how long it had been since he had looked after another European visitor. He had opened his mouth to answer and had then stopped, shaken his head and said he could not remember.

'This is why I am telling you we are so lucky. We have not had so much of European customer since 1989. But we have shops all over, in Srinagar and in all of top hotels in Delhi. Now with Manzoor travelling and doing so much of good work we are having business with America, France, Italy and UK. *Inshallah*, God has been great and good to us.' Saboor stopped for a moment. 'But you will see these ten years have been very bad for my people. You will see how much of suffering they have been having. Kashmiri peoples are not happy.' He looked out over the garden to the mountains and said no more.

I walked back through the flowers to my floating house. Moqbool was not on the boat. I sat out among the carved *chinar* leaves and watched the evening sun turn the mountains pale lavender and the clouds above the poplar trees pink. The house-boats on the other side of the lake glowed amber. A kingfisher flew through the carved pillars of the veranda and landed on a bleached branch just a few feet from where I sat. Its wings were bright, as bright as the lake was still, throwing back at the purple mountains a flawless image.

From beyond the silence of the lake and its fringing poplars came the sound of gunfire in the city.

'There are two things that you are going to become very familiar with in Kashmir,' said the officer who had been allocated to brief me as a journalist. He was a member of the BSF, the Border Security Force, based in Srinagar. We were sitting under a *chinar* tree in a garden beside Dal Lake that had been appropriated by the BSF seven years earlier.

'The first is gunfire. The second is that you are going to find the Kashmiri people no longer have any love for the Indian army. We have been here too long and I am afraid that the code of behaviour on both sides has slipped somewhat.' The officer was old school Indian army, well spoken, tall, thin and elegant in his uniform, the toes of his brown shoes polished to glass. He was keen to dissuade me from going out to any of the villages.

'I don't really see that it can be dangerous. I know your boys are all over the place. I'm hardly likely to be snatched from under the noses of the BSF.'

'Do not tempt fate, Miss Hardy,' he said as he waved to his bearer to bring another round of tea.

I had already drunk three cups. 'I'm so sorry but would it be possible to use your lavatory?' I asked.

The officer and the tea-carrying bearer looked at each other, momentarily bemused. Then a subaltern was called to my aid. He led the way to the main house. Ten years of military occupation had left their mark. Its windows were broken, its balconies fractured. My guide paused and, changing his mind, led me in another direction, towards a tented wall, hurrying ahead to shoo away the soldiers already using it. They hopped off, adjusting themselves and their flies. The subaltern waved me into an acrid open pissoir offering little privacy and then hovered at an almost suitable distance while I went behind the tenting.

'Are you still determined to stop me going out to the villages?' I asked the senior officer when I returned to the *chinar* tree.

'Miss Hardy, it is my experience that when an Englishwoman has made a decision there is not much a man can do to change her mind. You may go if it is your wish but please to return if any of my officers make such a request.' He paused. 'Something you must remember at all times.'

'What is that?'

'This is not a war of two sides. We are highly visible, they are not. And, Miss Hardy, we will not always be able to make lavatory arrangements out in the villages.' He smiled.

The BSF billet was just next door to Shalimar Bagh, one of the three Mogul gardens beside the lakes created by the Emperor Jahangir, his son Shah Jahan, and Jahangir's prime minister. They devised sanctuaries of tumbling water, flowers and fruit trees, and decreed pleasure domes to honour the beauty of their wives with avenues of fountains that led down to the lakes where the mountains were reflected.

The gardens are no longer Mogul retreats of polished lethargy. They are the property of the people of Kashmir and a testament to the dead hand of municipal supervision.

Shalimar Bagh was created by Jahangir for Nur Mahal, 'Light of the Palace', his famously beautiful wife. I went to see it again, to see if my imagination could stretch beyond the plastic bags in the clogged waterways and recall what had once been. It was not easy. Ten years of violence had raped the municipal council coffers. There were more plastic bags, fewer flowers and less grass.

The shikara *sign*

The main pavilion, in the process of being restored in 1992, was still shrouded in rusting corrugated iron. Only the great *chinar* trees still cast their dappled shade.

I sat down underneath one of them and was immediately distracted by a young couple doing what young couples do in public gardens in India. The sight was a familiar one. What had caught my eye was not the couple but those that watched. A group of soldiers sat in full combat gear, each bristling with weaponry, beneath the next *chinar* tree. And as they sat they made comments on the young couple's fumbling courtship.

Then a second group of soldiers crossed the garden with a local girl, heading in the direction of the public urinals. It was not clear who was leading and who was being led.

If I had not drunk so much tea with the BSF officer I would not have had to take the same route. I would not have seen the girl take one of the soldiers behind the padlocked ladies' lavatory. I would not have seen her come out again a couple of minutes later and take another soldier to the same place. I would not have heard the ugly things that the soldiers said as they gave her marks out of ten for her agility.

The ugliness of the relationship between the army and the local people in Srinagar makes itself felt at every turn, behind every tree in the Mogul gardens, around every street bunker. The soldiers do not want to be there and the Kashmiris do not want them there.

As I left, the gardeners came, trying to press flowers on me in the way they always had. At the steps below the garden, the *shik-aris* all jostled for business, competing for the young couples who were hoping to find a little more privacy than was available under the *chinar* trees of Shalimar Bagh.

CHAPTER 11

The Warped Weft

THE OFFICER UNDER the *chinar* tree by the lake had warned me but I still had plans beyond Srinagar. Though the *pashm* for our shawls came from *Capra hircus* goats in Ladakh, along the notoriously bad Srinagar-to-Leh road, there were still hundreds of cashmere goats in Kashmir to see. I wanted to go up into the mountains, to visit the herders to see how they had fared over the past ten years and particularly since the fighting around Kargil during the summer.

There are three kinds of hill herders in Kashmir, Chopans, Gujars and Bakarwals. The Chopans are the least nomadic. In summer they graze their herds up on the high *margs*, the alpine meadows of Kashmir, and in winter they return to their villages in the valleys. They do not like to be confused with the Gujars or Bakarwals. They are herders, they regard the others as gypsies. Chopans are still easily recognizable as Kashmiris in feature and dress.

It is the Gujars who are the real nomads of Kashmir. The valley people used to be frightened of these gypsy herders who from time to time descend from the high mountains with their herds, their wild songs and their strange language. Physically they are beautiful. The men are tall and lean, patrician in their looks. The younger women have eyes as big as their buffalo calves, and though they are as strong as their mules they are also somehow delicate at the same time. Gujars winter in the lower meadows and dry river-beds, setting up tented camps and causing merriment and a certain amount of trouble in the surrounding villages.

Bakarwals are Gujars from the Punjab. I could not tell the two groups apart until Salama, my guide, explained the difference. He had been appointed by the Wangnoo brothers as my protector. No one was happy about me heading for the hills, but we had compromised by my agreeing to be chaperoned. Salama was another of the Wangnoos' houseboat bearers, smaller than Moqbool but with the same carriage, the same greying beard. His chosen headpiece was a white *topi*, finely embroidered in gold with grapes and vine leaves. He told me proudly that it was not possible to get another one like it in the whole of Kashmir: it had been bought for him in Dubai. He had worked for the Wangnoos for thirty-five years and his younger brother was cook to all five of the houseboats.

As we made our way up into the mountains, Salama pointed out a Bakarwal. 'See, he is like gypsy, much more wild than Kashmiri Gujars.'

I smiled at the wild man and his herd of animals and laughing women. He flashed back white teeth, his walnut eyes alight and dancing.

Salama twitched his nose.

'These are rich peoples. Much more so than Kashmiri Gujars. See how much of sheeps and goats they are having, selling sheeps, selling goats and wool and some milk. They have much money. Kashmiri Gujars are poor peoples. They are not having much moneys. Only having some buffaloes and making little moneys from milk and sometimes little, little cheese.'

I had tasted the Gujars' cheese years before on my way to Amarnath when I met a group of them crossing a meadow and they gave me some of their soft curd cheese on a fig leaf. It had looked romantic but tasted bland.

Salama and I were travelling the road to Kargil where the war had started six months before. The silence of the lakes was replaced by the howling and belching of juggernauts on their way to or from Leh, fetching and carrying supplies before Ladakh was cut off by the first of the winter snows. Beyond the traffic on the road the fields of the valley stretched out, dotted here and there with poplars and *chinars*. It had rained the previous day, the first real rain for six months after a failed monsoon. The small plots of land were alive with bent bodies: men curled over wooden ploughs behind yawing teams of buffalo; women, their skirts hitched, digging potatoes and pulling carrots from the softened earth; and children, some helping but most hindering the work in progress.

Each field was shadowed by soldiers, black bandannas tied around their faces, guns across their chests. They stopped us whenever they had the chance, tension in the eyes that challenged us above the menace of the bandannas. They hit their guns against the door, saying nothing but demanding a lift. Each time, Salama jumped out of the jeep and stopped them from getting into the front with me, his tolerance pressed hard against the set of his teeth. Our driver remained silent, and conversation in the back between Salama and our temporary passengers was in Hindi, perfunctory and factual. Very few of the soldiers spoke Kashmiri. Nearly all of them were from regiments posted into the valley for the war – Sikhs from Punjabi regiments, Gurkhas with their *kukris* at their hips, sad almond-eyed Assamese Rifles – faces from all over India pulled into the valley in the cause of national security.

As we climbed up into the hills we dropped off our last passengers. They grunted as they got out of the car, no words, just sounds.

'This is only happening in these few years.' Salama gave a long sigh.

'I thought the army could always commandeer any private vehicle.'

'Maybe this is so but for first years there was much, much more of respect. I am saying this to you from my heart. In early years of army in Kashmir I am sometimes asking soldiers to help with things and they are agreeing and all of us Kashmiris are smiling. Here is army to protect us. Now it is all changed. They were once being fearful in case of militants being in cars or on buses. Now they are not caring, they just bang, bang their guns on any car or bus and it is having to stop and take them for ride. They know that it is making sadness in the Kashmiris. They do not care so much.'

A little further on another soldier flagged us down.

'See, they are thinking that it is game for stopping you because you are foreign lady with no husband for protecting,' said Salama.

But instead of rapping his gun against the door, the soldier knocked on the window. Then, before anything could be said, he waved his hand and pointed to a boy standing behind him, a local boy. He explained in fumbling Hindi that the boy hoped to get a lift to a village further up the valley. It was exactly where we were going. The lad hopped in with an ease that made it apparent he was quite used to cadging lifts using military traffic-stopping muscle.

There was a non-stop dialogue for the next twenty minutes between the boy and Salama. The boy talked of going to see his *mausī*, his aunt, but his innocence seemed contrived, his smile insincere. He was a child of the conflict, suckled on tension and educated by daily examples of the impermanence of life.

A group appeared from beneath some willows lining the road ahead of us. A local man, his hands tied on the top of his head, still in his pyjamas, his bedroll over his shoulder, familiar fear cut into his face, was being escorted by about twenty soldiers of the BSF. The boy gave us a running commentary. The man had been harbouring militants in his grain store. Worse than this, our informer elaborated, he had been transporting guns to Jammu in apple boxes, hidden under Kashmiri Delicious from his orchard.

We dropped our young veteran at Sonarmarg, once a favoured honeymoon resort and the location for any number of Bollywood films. The valley was now an extended military car park. The chalets where Bollywood's favourites had almost kissed were dressed in barbed wire, and hulks of military machinery blistered the close-grazed turf.

Our passenger did not seem keen to run off to see his *mausī*. He clung to us as we started to climb up towards the glacier at the head of the valley.

'Pony for nice lady?' he tried.

Salama muttered something to him but he was not so easily deterred.

'Am guiding for you.'

'I have a guide here with me, thank you.' I put my hand out to Salama.

The boy persisted. Salama scowled at him. The air was getting thinner and I was too busy catching my breath to be able to speak. I looked at the boy and smiled helplessly, shrugging my answers. When we paused for a rest he turned to look back down the valley. Another jeep was parking next to ours. The boy squinted into the sun to try and make out what the vehicle might offer and then turned away from us to go in search of other income. He had told me he was ten.

We climbed on in silence for a while. Salama was troubled.

'He will not have a good life. He is the kind that is going across the border,' he said sadly.

'What do you mean "across the border"?'

Salama was silent again. The expression was familiar. Lila had used it on the roof of the *Princess Grace* seven years before when she spoke of her cousin's disappearance.

'Have you heard stories about the children that disappear each year from villages in the hills?' I asked.

Salama stopped and looked fixedly up towards the glacier.

'We have been reading these stories in past years.'

'But have you heard anything recently?' I had found my second wind.

'Maybe it was happening some years ago but it is not happening now. Perhaps some were being taken from villages and some were going on their own. But this not happening in Srinagar, never from Srinagar.' He shook his head at the peaks.

'I'm not sure I understand what you mean about them going on their own.'

Lila had made it very clear that her cousin had not gone willingly.

'I will tell you something but you must be sure to understand what I am saying. Some boy taking study in same school as older of my sons was talking to my son and telling things to him about going across the border for joining with militants. My son is coming to me and telling me these things. I am putting my hand to my heart and saying to him that this boy is from bad family. I say to my son, look at what he has with us, his family. If he is wanting to join militants there is nothing I can do to stop him from this. Please to hear this right way but I am having tears in my eyes when I am saying this to my son.' Salama started to walk on ahead of me. I could not see his face as he spoke.

'My son is telling to me that he would never do this thing. He is saying to me in name of Allah that he would never be leaving the family for this thing. This is the promise that I take from him and I am believing, *inshallah*.' His voice dropped away.

'Do you mean that a lot of these children are going of their own free will because it means that they can get away from their families?'

hand and traced the lines on my palm, laughing at the blue veins on my wrist. A woman appeared behind her, her face a softer version of the Chopan's, an older version of the child's. They were a family – daughter, mother and brother.

We sat outside their tent and Salama patiently translated my questions.

They had come down from the high pastures and were on their way back to their village in the valley where they would spend the winter. It had been a bad summer.

'Why?' I asked.

'The army were not letting us use our summer pastures. We had to move on all the time. The animals are not carrying enough fat now for the winter. We will have to cut food for them all through the snows.'

A tiny shivering lamb wobbled towards us, bleating. The Chopan picked it up and pushed it into the warmth of his *feron*. The bleating stopped.

Salama explained that most of the summer pastures were up around Kargil, about a hundred miles away.

The Chopan's sister brought out flat bowls of mountain tea, twice-boiled goat's milk flavoured with tea stems. Salama sucked at a hookah that the Chopan had passed to him. The little girl started playing with my rucksack. My passport fell from one of its pockets. The Chopan retrieved it from the dirt and turned it over in his hands.

'He is asking if you can travel anywhere in the world with this,' Salama translated.

'Almost anywhere. They say we will be able to use them for the moon too.'

At that the Chopan laughed. Then he opened the passport, flicking through the pages until he came to the photograph at the very end. He stared at it for a long time before producing a leather pouch from inside his *feron*. He took out his identity card. In it was a photograph, together with his name, his

village, his date of birth and his Jammu and Kashmir registra-
tion number. Then it showed his profession. The cashmere
herders of the valley have now become 'government meat
suppliers'.

'He is saying that it is only possible for him to get to Srinagar
and Jammu with this,' Salama explained.

The Chopan stopped for a moment.

'He is saying that he does not believe there would be too
much of grazing on moon,' Salama laughed.

We walked back to the main path through the Chopan's
herd of leggy sheep and long-fleeced goats, cashmere goats.
I stopped to feel the coat of one of them but she twisted away
from my touch. The next minute I was lying spread-eagled in
the dirt, floored by a billy defending his harem. Winded, I lay
there, the Chopan's laughter ringing in my ears, in my hand a
tuft of goat fleece softer than baby's down.

I returned to Srinagar to find a note from Manzoor on the
dining-room table of the houseboat.

'Greetings and good morning to you. I am arrived from
Delhi. I have many things to show. You will love them. Come
to office in afternoon. We will take tea. There is much to speak
of.'

When I arrived Manzoor seemed to be on three telephones
at once. Wangnoo brother number one, guardian of the empire,
was busy. Two weavers stood at his desk, waiting to take orders,
waiting to be paid. In the summer room outside the office, four
embroiderers sat hunched over test pieces, waiting for judgement to be passed on their work. I sat in front of Manzoor's
desk, happy to take my turn. A young man came up the garden
with two large rolled carpets bouncing on each shoulder.
Manzoor jumped up to inspect them. Thousands of pounds'

Salama with the Chopan's hookah

worth of silk carpet were laid out on the grass, squinted at, walked on, rubbed and sniffed, and then accepted. The carpets went away and now it was the embroiderers' turn. Manzoor was on the phone to the Jammu and Kashmir tourist department, arranging for a map to be made of the route from the airport to the houseboats while signing a cheque for one weaver and writing down an order for the other. He wrote in a book, the kind that has been used in India since the British first gave the nation advanced bureaucracy and double-entry book-keeping. He wrote on the rough paper with a Mont Blanc pen that was perfectly in tune with his Pringle socks peeping out from under the undyed cotton of his *feron*.

He looked up from his book.

'Just two minutes, dear, and I will be finished.'

The embroiderers submitted their samples and went home, the weavers took their cheques and orders. Manzoor, Ashraf and I were left alone in the office. But there was another figure sitting quietly in the corner, head bent over his paperwork. It was Yaseen, patient and waiting. When all the artisans had gone he came forward and shook my hand, his expression calm and soothing amid the feverish activity.

'I am confused, Manzoor. I thought you were bringing *pashm* out of Ladakh yourself.'

'Who is saying this?' he asked.

'You did, but I have just watched all the woven pashmina coming straight from the weavers.'

'This is so. It comes straight from weavers, straight from Ladakh, I am not lying to you.' He jumped up and crossed to a piece of framed script on the wall behind my head. 'See, look at this. You will love this.'

Underneath the Arabic was an English translation. 'An honest trader will always walk with the Prophet . . .'

Manzoor spread his hands in front of him.

'This is what I believe, this is how I am running our business as elder brother. Believe me, have you not just seen many peoples coming, going, coming in this office? And you have been here just few minutes. Imagine how many peoples are coming here in a week, a month. I, my family, our business, we are helping many, many hundreds of peoples all over, weavers of shawl, weavers of carpet, makers of papier mâché, carvers of walnut, many, many peoples and many families. I am paying for school with more than two hundred childrens. This is my honest wish. Mohammed is telling us five things – belief, prayer, fasting, giving to poor and making *haj*. This is my belief, this is belief of all my family.' Manzoor was standing in front of the piece of script, his hands in the air as he delivered his sermon.

On the table in front of me, underneath a Kashmiri samovar, was a copy of a news magazine that Manzoor had obviously brought from Delhi. Its lead story screamed alarming details of the militants who had infiltrated Kashmir, supposedly with the backing of Pakistan. I picked up the magazine.

Manzoor waved his hand at the cover.

'This is what is giving me so much of sadness. This is not us, this is not how we believe, this is not what we are wanting. Why are they doing this thing? Why are they putting this story like this? You are a journalist, you are seeing what is happening to my peoples because of this. You think this is what we are wanting?' All the laughter had gone from his voice.

Two telephones rang. Manzoor picked them both up, one to each ear.

I looked at Ashraf who had been watching his elder brother, a slightly amused expression on his face.

'Would you like *Azadi* for Kashmir?' I asked.

'*Azadi*, what does it mean to me? It is meaning nothing if I am being told to sit in my house with my family and shut all the doors, shut out the light and the life. *Azadi* is not freedom if it means my people are hungry and in suffering. What time do we have on earth? Maybe fifty, sixty, maybe eighty years, *inshallah*. This is not so much of time. Why to spend it in hunger and pain? *Azadi* for us is to feel safe, to feel free, to be able to go where we want to, free to let our daughters be walking in the streets, free to be able to do business making whatever is our thing and making enough of profit to be as it was before all of this.' He clenched his fist in his lap.

Manzoor put down both receivers and interrupted.

'How can we have *Azadi*? How would we protect ourselves? What do we have in our beautiful valley? Ahmed, brother of my grandfather, was very much liking proverb: "There are three things which ease the heart from sorrow – water, green grass and the beauty of women." But my good uncle was saying we have all these things in Kashmir yet we are still poor. All things we are needing are coming from India. We need India.' He turned for a moment from his topic, giving instructions to Yaseen and Ashraf, shouting to Saboor in the next room and to another boy in the room beyond. 'Come, we are going to see weavers.'

As we drove through the back lanes of Srinagar I counted the women on the road. Of the forty we passed thirty-two were in the full *burqa*, skin, hair, eye colour, shape, age and expression hidden beneath black billows. I did not remember there being so many Kashmiri women under the veil on my last visit.

Manzoor saw me watch a group of blue-jeaned boys staring at a group of girls, some veiled, some bare-faced, as they walked past. There was a lot of leering. Manzoor lifted both hands from the wheel in too narrow a street.

'See this thing. I worry so much for my childrens. There is so much of change in atmosphere here in these ten years. This is not a good place for my childrens to be growing. This is why I am spending so much of money to be sending them all to college in Manchester, *inshallah*. You are seeing there is so much of dirtiness in the street, even for womens and girls in the veil.' He lurched out of the path of a tonga and turned into an even narrower side alley where he waited patiently while an old man in the road ahead squatted down and urinated into an open drain. Once he had finished the man was given a rousing blast from our horn to clear him out of the road. Then Manzoor parked so that I had to step into the same open drain to get out of the car.

He ushered me through an outer door, across an inner court-yard, down a dark passage and through a low doorway. Old shuttered windows looked out over a second courtyard, with dark timber buildings beyond. Delicate carved balconies were suspended from the upper storeys, and through their wooden lattice-work was a view of Haramukh, the highest peak in the Vale of Kashmir.

In front of a window off the courtyard a figure sat behind a pash-mina loom, silhouetted by white light, penned in by the delicate walls of warp and weft that he wove. As he spoke to Manzoor his head remained bent to the loom, his hands still busy with their work.

'He is saying that rain of last night has made it clear and he is seeing the great peak for first time for many months. He is taking this as message that it is time for taking his good wife on *umra*,' Manzoor explained.

'*Umra?*' I asked.

'Is pilgrimage to Mecca when it is not time of *haj*. This man is taking himself and his wife for *umra* every year. He is weaving, weaving, and when he has enough of money he is waiting for sign to take *umra*. Now he is having sign he will be making plans for departure.'

The weaver's wife sat in the corner of the room, wooden frames of fine yarn about her feet. Her hands danced between two spindles, winding on *pashm*. Fragments floated from her fingers, drifting in the currents of air. From the window, from beneath her husband's hands, came a constant whisper. It was

'Penned in by the delicate walls of warp and weft that he wove'

the flight of the shuttle as he threw it from hand to hand through the warp on the loom. I crouched down beside him. With the light behind me I could see the detail of his work and I caught the sun in the corners of his wife's cracked smile as she saw me watching her husband's feet on the wooden pedals of the loom, his toes curled and curved to their shape. They moved to the same dance as his wife's hands between the spindles. I reached out to touch the woven piece the old man was rolling off his loom, pure Kashmiri pashmina, air and strength. Though there was movement all around him, the old man's eyes flew only with his shuttle. I thanked him for letting us disturb him. He nodded his head without looking up, his eyes on the shuttle, his mind on his *umra* and the clear view to Haramukh peak. We left him to his work.

Manzoor twisted to try and unlock the passenger car door without having to step in the open drain.

'Who is parking car this way?' he asked, looking at me in surprise.

I shrugged.

He was quiet as we drove back towards the house by the lake. He broke the silence just as we reached it.

'There is so much of artistry in Kashmir and it is all locked up by these ten years. Slowly, slowly we will find ways of setting it free again, *inshallah*.' He stopped carefully, giving me plenty of room to negotiate the puddle he had used as a parking spot.

That night Moqbool served me lotus root, the first of the autumn from the lake, in a great brass-covered dish at my single place in the middle of the long carved dining-room table. He talked as I ate. *Wuzmal* had only been finished the year before and the Wangnoos had been forced to pay three times the real price for the cedarwood from which it was made because of the militants' stranglehold on the timber trade.

I had seen the disenchanted groups of young people hanging around on street corners in the city day after day as I made my way about. Ten years earlier eighty per cent of the people in Srinagar had worked in jobs directly related to tourism. Now there were no jobs. The young school-leavers and graduates were angry.

'You are a father, Moqbool, how do you stop your children from joining the militants when they are recruiting so effectively from among young people in the city?'

'My son is just ten years.'

He poured more water into my glass and reorganized the dishes on the table around my place, then resumed his position in front of the china cupboard.

'My brothers, both more young than me, were working in restaurant in old city. One brother is coming to house and saying he is up and off to Pakistan to train with militants. They were coming to him and other brother in restaurant and saying many stories about good life in Pakistan. We are saying no, this thing you must not do. Sit in house, no go to work and wait for passing time. I am reminding them of *mausī* who was going Peshawar side with husband in times before Partition. Number one son of *mausī* was coming to Srinagar maybe eleven years back. He was looking around him in this place and saying "You have heaven." I am asking him what he means. He was saying to me that in Peshawar there was fighting all of times, not enough food, not enough of all things. He was carrying gun at all times, all boys carrying guns. Then he is going back to Pakistan and we are hearing nothing of him and his family. Then we are hearing stories of all being killed.'

'Why would they have been killed?'

'Because *mausī* and husband were of Kashmir. This thing I am saying to my brothers. Slowly, slowly they are staying in house and deciding not to go with militants.' Moqbool stared out of the window.

I finished eating in the silence of his thoughts. Then he picked up the plates and turned to me at the door.

'You must be writing these things. All stories of Kashmir are bad stories. How much of this are we to have?'

'I will try.'

'You will try, *inshallah*.' He walked away down the corridor, his footsteps heavy with the uncertainty of my understanding. The boat creaked in reply.

CHAPTER 12

Tea without Mr Butt

THERE HAD BEEN heavy rain all through the night and the mountains were clear, the haze washed away. Drops of water lay on the lotus leaves, as perfect and silvered as mercury. The rain had also ushered in the beginning of autumn. Leaves had begun to turn in the night, the first flashes of copper, the same burnished glow as in the samovar shops of the old city.

Among dead stems staring at the sky with empty eyes, the lotus-pickers dragged their small flat boats, hooking roots to feed the people of Srinagar through the winter. A girl in a lavender head-scarf crouched on the front of her boat, looking out through the stems. She was beautiful, with pale skin, high cheekbones, light brown eyes and dark brown curly hair escaping from the edges of her scarf. Then she smiled, showing ragged teeth and a lot of gum, her beauty suddenly broken.

I was in search of the Butts. Sudij the boatman stopped when I called out to him. There, on the edge of the lotuses, next to an overgrown floating garden, listing gently to one side, was a house-boat. She had been repainted pale green and most of her windows were now broken, but I recognized the *Princess Grace*. Sudij pushed us through the weeds to her side. The doors were open. Inside, all the furniture had gone and her carved sitting-room walls had become darkened by smoke. I called out.

A woman came from the back of the boat. I did not recognize her. Sudij translated for me. The woman's husband had bought the *Princess Grace* five years before. She did not know anything about the Butt family. She turned away to hang out the wet clothes draped over her arm. I called to her in the few words of Kashmiri I knew, smiling and pleading. She spoke to Sudij again. She thought that perhaps one of the daughters of the family had married a copper merchant who lived somewhere near Shah-i-Hamdan mosque in the old city. As we pushed off I could see through a window into the room that I had slept in seven years before. It was almost bare, with just some sacking on the floor and several bedrolls around the edge beneath the cracked stained-glass windows and carved ceiling where I had dreamt of Mogul gardens.

Shah-i-Hamdan mosque is the oldest in Srinagar and has no minarets or domes. It is just a simple wooden building, its timbers dovetailed with all the skill of a cabinet-maker, without glue or nails. 'Non-Muslims or Ladies not to proceed beyond this gate' read the sign above the soldier's head at the doorway. A man at the donation box eyed my plump handbag and let me go up to a little window next to the door to look inside.

Shah Hamdan's followers introduced Islam to Kashmir in the fourteenth century. The mosque had been built in his memory. Through my peep-hole I looked on to a spread of carpets and, above them, a canopy of brass chandeliers. A father and his two small sons were the only ones at prayer, kneeling and bowing in unison. The soldier tapped me on the shoulder – the non-Muslim had seen enough. I fed the donation box and asked the man beside it where I would find the street where most of the copper merchants had their shops. He waved me toward Zen Kadl, one of the seven bridges across the Jhelum river in the old city.

All the animals in the old city seemed to be dying. Dogs with swollen rib cages lay curled in corners. Ancient cloudy-eyed *tonga* ponies stood in the central reservation of the main

The entrance to Shah-i-Hamdan mosque

road, their heads drooping with exhaustion. Chickens with bare necks wallowed in the dust. The streets were still but it was not a peaceful quiet, more a heavy pause, an intake of breath. I was in the Hindu quarter, its empty streets lined with beautiful eighteenth-century merchants' houses, their balconies and carved shutters reaching, layer upon layer, up towards the sky. But there were no roofs. Every single house had been burnt out by the militants. The Hindus were long gone, leaving behind only the blackened skeletons of their once prosperous businesses. Their shopfronts had been boarded up and were now covered in graffiti, ugly threats scrawled by various militant groups, all united in their loathing of the Hindus. Once they had run the most successful businesses and dominated local government jobs.

In Shah Hamdan Street I stood in the middle of the road, staring through empty, charred casements. A solitary cyclist, loaded with winter greens, rang his bell to move me. It sounded loud in the silence. I would not even have heard it on a street in the new city on the other side of town.

At the first copper shop on the street leading away from Zen Kadl I stopped and asked a shrivelled man, squatting among his samovars, if he knew of a merchant who had married Lila Butt, the houseboat-owner's daughter from Nagin. He looked at me with the same rheumy eyes as the *tonga* ponies and bubbled his hookah. As I admired his glowing goods he called out to someone inside the shop. I heard him say Lila's name. A woman appeared at the door, as fat as her husband was thin, round faced and round hipped under a grey woollen tunic. She came to the front of the shop and reached out to touch my face. Then she climbed down the step at the front with difficulty and led me along the street to another shop, almost identical to that of her husband, except that it was half the size. It was at the bottom of a narrow wooden house with latticed wooden shutters. Some of the glass in the windows was broken and one corner of the building was sinking into its foundations. A small girl looked out of one of the upstairs windows. Her hair was light brown and she had smoky blue eyes.

I thanked the woman who had directed me but she would not leave. She wanted to know why I wanted to see a copper merchant's wife. She called to the girl at the window. Another face appeared, a taller, dark-eyed boy. He was not as shy as his little sister and he waved and called out to me. A woman's face came out of the dark interior behind him, but I did not recognize her until she shouted my name. It was Lila.

She registered the pause before I smiled and called back to her. She knew that I had not recognized her and she pulled back from the window into the shadows. We both knew. In seven years Lila had changed, almost beyond recognition. Then she had been seventeen. She was twenty-four now. I heard her weight on the stairs inside the house. There was another pause before she opened the door. I could sense her putting her hand to her hair, a moment of pain because she knew how much she had altered and she knew she was going to see it reflected in my face.

She took my hand between both of hers. The skin was rough and her nails were short, ragged and dirty. Her face and her body were swollen. Putting my hand to her stomach, I smiled at her pregnancy.

'A baby, when is it due?' I asked.

Lila pushed my hand away.

'No baby, just big and fat now.' She saw the older copper merchant's wife standing behind me and scowled.

'She helped me to find you,' I explained.

Lila and the woman had a rapid conversation at full volume. The woman eventually nodded and looked at me, her eyebrows forming question marks.

'What did you say to her?' I asked.

Lila was laughing, seventeen again.

'She was asking me what *farangi* unmarried woman is wanting with me. So I am saying to her that you are coming to me as friend

232

for help for finding nice Kashmiri husband.' Her whole face was alight and she laughed until she reached out for the door-post to keep her balance.

'Come,' she offered, as she caught her breath for a moment.

Lila stepped aside to let me in. Her two children were hanging in her shadow behind the door. The little girl scuttled away but the boy stood his ground, reaching out his hand and shaking mine, a grave expression on his face. He could not have been more than five.

'How are you?' he said in a small, serious voice.

'Very well, thank you. Lila, you're teaching them English already.'

She shrugged and kissed the top of her son's head.

'Not so much, I am not speaking so much now.'

As quickly as her laughter had come, it was gone. She waved me up some stairs and I could hear her laboured breathing behind me as we climbed. She was a young woman but it was as if the Lila that I had met on Nagin Lake was now buried underneath seven years of unhappiness, thickly padded with a heaviness of flesh and spirit.

In a semi-dark room above her husband's copper shop, Lila told me of the past seven years. I could not see her properly in the weak light but the shadows seemed to give her the freedom to speak as her children climbed over her, peering at me, asking her questions, demanding food, water and her attention in the face of an intruder. Lila cuddled them, brushed them away or shouted at them in turn, depending on how far she had got in her story.

She had married just after her eighteenth birthday. She did not elaborate on her wedding. When I asked her about her husband she shrugged. He was not Mr Butt's friend whose brother had business interests in America. I was going to ask more but I could feel Lila looking at me in the half-light, her eyes begging me not to question her. She asked if I wanted tea and then left the room. There was no one except Lila to make the tea.

I was alone with her son, Imran. The little girl had gone with Lila, clinging to her mother's *kameez*. Imran came closer. He was his mother as she had been when I first met her, individual, wilful and thin as a lotus stem. He asked me questions in Kashmiri and seemed frustrated when I could only smile or give inadequate one-word answers that made little sense. There were simple questions I longed to be able to ask him, things that I felt I probably could not ask Lila. Where was his father? Why was the shop closed?

I was asking him how old he was when Lila came back into the room, the girl, Suriya, still clinging to her. Lila waited for Imran to reply. She smiled when he did so in his quiet, solemn voice. Then he stepped towards me and reached out for the watch on my wrist. Lila shouted at him but he stood his ground, his hand on my watch, his mother's son. She pinched his ear gently, proud and embarrassed. Then she poured tea, sweet *dudh chai*, the same as we had drunk in the Butt family *dunga* seven years before when Lila was going to marry a rich man who would take her away from the lake and give her servants and time to while away. She was no longer by the lake and she was still drinking *dudh chai*. The rest had not gone according to plan.

Lila handed me a cup. It was one of the set that I had drunk tea from on the *Princess Grace*, a delicate, flowered cup with a handle too small to hold in any other way than between two fingers.

'I saw *Princess Grace* near the lotus garden. Did your father sell her to the floating gardener?' I remembered Mr Butt talking of getting a new boat made, as he had picked the most succulent pieces of lamb from an untouched dish at the dining-table, while he sat cross-legged beside me in a large walnut carver chair.

'Chāchājī, my uncle, was selling it to the gardener.' Lila stared into her cup.

The little girl started to cry. Lila gathered her into her bosom.

I was about to ask why but Lila spoke over my question.

'Very bad things were happening to my family. Police came to take Pitājī in '92. People were telling bad stories about him.

Burnt-out shells in the Hindu quarter of old Srinagar

Stories, stories, such stories of how he was giving help to militants because he was still making so much of business, even in bad times, with peoples like yourself coming. You were knowing Pitājī, you are knowing how much he is hating all of militants and so forth.'

I remembered Mr Butt banging his fist on the table between the rice and the fried ladies' fingers, raging about the militants and the havoc they were wreaking on the valley. I remembered Mr Butt thanking Allah that he had no son to lose to the militants. That, he said, would break his heart.

But it was not the militants who broke Mr Butt's heart. He had a heart attack while he was in police detention. Lila said it was because they had made threats. His family would suffer if he did not give them information and his houseboats would be black-listed.

'What was he to say to this? He was not knowing anything,' Lila shouted, pulling her daughter to her so that she started to cry again.

Mr Butt had not died at the police station. He had lived for another six months until just after Lila's wedding. Before her father's arrest Lila had been engaged to her father's friend, the one with the brother with American business interests. When her father was taken by the police her plump, middle-aged fiancé called off the engagement.

'He wasn't much of a friend. He must have known that your father was not involved in anything to do with the militants.'

'In Srinagar in '91 and '92 no one was having any friends. You were seeing how much trouble there was. Pitājī was making business and other peoples were having no business. Everyone, friend or no friend, was talking, telling stories about peoples who were having business. Friends? There were no friends.' She brushed Imran away as he tried to cuddle up beside Suriya. Lila was angry.

After her engagement had been broken off her uncle found her another fiancé very quickly. This time there were no frills. He was a copper merchant from the old city, shunned by other families because his shop was on one of the streets where the militants had burnt out so many of the old Hindu houses. At the time the Hindu area of old Srinagar was the most dangerous place in Kashmir. Lila had married the copper merchant after a short engagement. She had spent the first week of her marriage at her new husband's home as was the custom. Then she had returned to her family for a week before starting out on the rest of her married life. Mr Butt had died the day after Lila had gone back home, on her eighteenth birthday in April 1993. Lila's return to her new married home had been delayed for a month while they had buried and mourned her father.

'Pitājī was saying to me on day of marriage that he was not giving things to me that he was wanting to give. I am crying and saying to him that he has been giving me all of things, jewellery for my marriage and food and home while I am growing. He is saying that it is this thing that has broken his heart.' Lila rubbed her eyes like a little girl to stop herself from crying. 'Are you understanding this? He was dying because of things he was hating more than all other things. He was hating militants, and peoples were saying he was with them all of the time he was dying.' Now she was crying, her tears falling on the little girl in her lap.

We sat in that small room listening to Lila's tears until she was quiet.

'How are your mother and Aban?' I asked through the weight of silence.

Lila looked confused for a moment. Then she pulled herself together.

'Staying with Chāchājī, my uncle.'

I did not need to ask whether Aban was married. Lila, the prize, was married to a poor copper merchant. Aban would be twenty-one and unmarried. Single is not a word used to describe Kashmiri Muslim women. They are either girls, unmarried, or married women.

'Where does your uncle live?'

'In Srinagar, close by to University of Kashmir and Hazrat Bal mosque.' Within sight of Nagin Lake, where they had been happy on the Butt houseboats.

'Did your uncle sell the *Princess Diana* and the *Queen Noor* as well?' I asked of the other two boats in the former empire of Mr Butt.

'*Queen Noor* is on Dal Lake, maybe for me or Aban when times are not so bad. *Princess Diana* Chāchājī was selling for breaking carvings for other boats. *Princess Grace* was being sold for hospital, for medicines for Pitājī and for making of my . . .' Lila drank her tea without finishing her sentence. She did not need to tell me that some of the money would have been needed to buy her dowry jewellery and gold.

I remembered Mr Butt standing proudly at the dining-table, a piece of spicy lotus root between his finger and thumb.

'For marriage of Lila all my boats will light whole of Nagin Lake. Everyone will be coming to her marriage.' He had glowed at the thought as he ate the lotus root. 'So good for you, lotus root. You must eat more of. Very good for heart and problems of the chest,' he had said, as more went into his mouth.

I had not had much opportunity since then to eat lotus root and it had not been good enough to save Mr Butt.

'And Aban is well?' I asked Lila.

She did not answer. I thought she had not heard me so I asked again. She shouted to the children to go to the kitchen for *kulcha*, the dry biscuits of Kashmir.

'Aban has done many bad things since death of Pitājī. Please not to speak of this.'

I didn't press her but I couldn't help thinking of the local girl in Shalimar Bagh with the soldiers and of sweet Aban, her eyes flecked with light.

Lila had said nothing about her husband. I asked where he was.

'At market at Jami Masjid, selling all of copper things to ladies.'

Light through the wooden interior of Jami Masjid, the Friday Mosque

The market outside Jami Masjid swells on Friday afternoons after prayers, when the women of Srinagar go to shop in the shadow of their oldest mosque, in safety.

'Is he a good husband?' I asked her with a smile, meaning it lightly as women's talk.

Lila did not reply but pulled both her children to her again. Imran dodged away, more interested in eating *kulcha* than in cuddling his mother.

A dark shape appeared at the doorway, a woman in the full *burqa*, ageless and faceless. Lila introduced us. The woman was her mother-in-law. She lifted her veil and beneath the anonymous black her features seemed pinched and fat at the same time. She smiled generously at me and seemed happy to sit watching as Lila and I talked. But though she was warm towards me, her relationship with Lila appeared uncomfortable. Lila was the larger presence in the small house and her mother-in-law's dislike of this tip of the balance was tangible. She cuddled her grandchildren but turned her body away from Lila or failed to hear her when she spoke, not directly rude but cold. For her part Lila seemed louder when her mother-in-law was in the room, exerting herself both vocally and physically. Then the older woman asked Lila to go and get more tea. There was no choice but for her to do so.

When she had gone the old woman and I sat staring at each other. Her smile was still warm though there was a sense of confusion behind it. What was this foreigner doing with her son's wife, appearing unannounced at his house when he was not there? She took in every detail, my lack of jewellery, my clothes, my bare feet and particularly my ringless left hand. It was as though she was storing it all away for later, to be pulled out again and picked over once I had gone, once her son was there and the balance was back in her favour.

Lila returned with a samovar and one cup and put them in front of her mother-in-law. Carefully she poured out the tea, added sugar and stirred it slowly before handing it to the matriarch of the house. Her mother-in-law took one sip and put the cup down, reaching out to her grandson to help her to her feet. She smiled at me again and left the room without saying anything.

Lila beat her fist against her forehead. Imran and Suriya were fighting over my watch. Lila snatched it from them and handed it back to me.

'Have you made marriage?' she asked, a brittle smile on her sad face.

'No, Lila, I haven't, but I've been doing lots of other things.'

'Have you been going to America?'

'Yes, I went to Los Angeles.'

Lila was wide-eyed.

'Is this thing true that ladies in this place are having plastic . . .' Lila pointed to her generous bosom, laughing.

'Absolutely, it is the passport to life in Los Angeles. They thought I was very strange because I had hung on to my originals for more than thirty years.'

Lila rocked with laughter, but then stopped mid-breath.

'Are you saying that they are cutting them off?' Her face was frozen in horror.

'Not exactly, no, they don't cut them off but they do cut them open.'

Lila looked disgusted. 'This thing is making me think that I am very happy I was not going to America.' Then she stopped laughing. 'Why are you coming again to Kashmir?'

'I came to buy shawls, pashmina shawls.'

She looked at me closely, not understanding. For the first time I noticed the deep lines either side of her mouth, so marked even in the fullness of her face.

'I buy shawls here and sell them in England. Most of the profit goes to some schools in Delhi, in the slum areas. A friend of mine runs an NGO that tries to help educate children and adults in some of the slums where they cannot get basic education.'

Lila looked more confused.

'You are selling shawls in London? Who is buying shawls?' she asked.

'Rich women who are interested in India.'

'If they are interested, why are they not coming here to Kashmir?'

'Because rich people like to buy things from people who have spent a long time finding the best and the most beautiful. The more unusual something is, the more money they are happy to pay.'

There was a bemused expression on Lila's face.

'Are they wearing much of jewellery?' she asked.

I thought of the loud New Yorker at her sushi and muffin party, her scruffy clothes set off by huge diamonds in her ears, of Alessandra, the beautiful Italian girl in her leather sitting-room in Eaton Square, a solitaire floating at her throat, of the Cartier and carat-branded women who had flicked through shawls at countless sales and showings.

'Yes, I suppose they are.'

'And they must be beautiful, all of them?' Lila looked at her stubby fingernails.

'Some of them are, but quite a lot of them buy it.'

'Buy beautiful, how are you buying beautiful?'

'They will buy a pashmina shawl from me and then wrap themselves up in it. That makes them feel beautiful.'

'And you are selling shawls to them for making money for children in Delhi?'

'Yes.'

Lila put her arm around Suriya.

'What happened to your *mauserāi bhāi*, your cousin Azad who was taken from the village?'

Lila's smoky blue eyes closed and she pulled Suriya closer to her.

'It is more than ten years, he is all gone now.' She fiddled with her daughter's hair and did not look at me.

I had something to give Lila. I took it out of my bag and

handed it to her. It was one of the finest pashminas I had been able to buy from Manzoor, one hundred per cent Kashmiri pashmina woven by the old man beside his view of Haramukh peak. It was the same soft brown as the donkey foals in the cricket meadow below the Wangnoos' house. All around the edge it was embroidered in fine silk, the pale lavender of the mist on the mountains on a hazy day, the green of the willow trees and the washed gold of the poplars as they began to turn with the first of the cold nights of autumn. It was her wedding present, given six years too late.

Lila opened the packet and sat staring at it. Then she lifted it out of its tissue wrapping and pulled off her grey wool shawl. Her face was frozen and her silence filled the room as she gazed at the embroidery, her blue eyes happy again as I remembered they had been seven years before when she had talked of the fine marriage she would make. She pulled the shawl around herself and Suriya and then looked up at me.

'Why are you not giving the money from our pashmina shawls to children of Kashmir?'

I could smell the cardamom and cinnamon from the samovar of tea that Lila had made for her mother-in-law. In the grey light of that room it had a melancholy scent.

I had no answer for Lila.

I left the ghosts of Zen Kadl and flew back into vibrant London, humming with the magnetic swipe of millions of credit cards.

Delicate white Christmas fairy lights made discreet starbursts among small fir trees along the elegant shopping streets of Notting Hill, where pashmina wearers roamed. The shawls had become the common uniform of the street where, just two years before, I had been stopped in the rain by an American woman in a tight white jersey because of the novelty of my shawl.

Goats on the mountainside

This time I was wearing a shawl that I had bought the week before from one of our embroiderers in the back streets of Srinagar. His initials were in the corner, SoK, Star of Kashmir, as Manzoor had nicknamed him because of the exquisite intricacy of his work. The shawl was the colour of champagne held to the sun. It was embroidered in silk, the work of one man for four months, the stitching so fine that I could hardly tell the difference between the front and the back, tiny flowers and paisley curling one into the other across the whole length. It was a wedding shawl.

A voice called across the street. 'Still flogging those things? I love what you're wearing. Are you selling those now?' It was a woman wrapped in a plain pashmina silk that she had bought from me the previous year. 'I hope they're not too much. You know everyone's selling them for half the price they were last year?' She flicked expensive hair over her lavender shawl. 'Look at them, they're everywhere, even after that *Vogue* RIP pashmina piece. Did you see it?'

'No, I've been in Kashmir.'

'God, that's brave. Aren't they still fighting a war?' She retreated further into her lavender folds.

'They never really stopped fighting.'

I had not been brave. I had been impotent in a place desperate for voices braver than mine. I was buying shawls from weavers who clung to their craft in the terrorist twilight of their valley. I was giving money to slum projects in Delhi, to unfamiliar faces, when children of people I knew and had stayed with in Kashmir had been taken from their families and never found. I was selling shawls made by the descendants of Mogul artisans to women with a weakness for cappuccino and a horror of cellulite who open their cheque books generously but wearily as I tell the story.

And the children of the weavers hang around on the streets of Srinagar, unable to find work. They listen to the fighting talk of the militants and they like the idea of having a gun in their hands and a cause into which they can channel their anger and their confusion. I buy shawls, and families like the Wangnoos make money that enables them to send their children to Islamic schools abroad, where they believe the purity of the teachings of the Koran cannot be sullied by internecine war.

While the guns fire on the streets of Srinagar, and in the mountains that look down into the valley, the lakes will remain silent, empty of the trade that gave Kashmir a voice and a gentler quality of life before 1989. And while another child from a Delhi slum is given a basic education and a voice, the mothers of Kashmir, who sons have joined the militants, cry silently.

On the street in Notting Hill, the woman in her lavender Kashmiri pashmina smiled a Christmas shopping smile to close the conversation and walked on by.

Acknowledgements

I WOULD LIKE to thank, above all, the ordinary people of Kashmir, whose livelihood has been put in constant jeopardy since 1989, for their warmth and hospitality. My thanks too to Paddy Singh, Alka Kohli and the Government of India Tourist Office for helping me get into Kashmir, the Wangnoo family, the Butt family, and Rajiv, my friend and hero in Delhi. Between the two countries and the two cultures, thank you David. In England I would like to thank Natasha Fairweather at A.P. Watt, Gail Pirkis at John Murray for wisdom and surgery, and Jill Langford for the photograph of Robin on p. 91.

Lastly, my thanks to Richard for his constant quiet support, and of course, to all the ladies who have bought pashmina from Goat.